William Conway

With Ski & Sledge over Arctic Glaciers

William Conway

With Ski & Sledge over Arctic Glaciers

ISBN/EAN: 9783743319387

Manufactured in Europe, USA, Canada, Australia, Japa

Cover: Foto ©Andreas Hilbeck / pixelio.de

Manufactured and distributed by brebook publishing software (www.brebook.com)

William Conway

With Ski & Sledge over Arctic Glaciers

WITH SKI & SLEDGE
OVER ARCTIC GLACIERS

BY

SIR MARTIN CONWAY

ILLUSTRATED FROM PHOTOGRAPHS
TAKEN BY E. J. GARWOOD

LONDON
J. M. DENT & CO.
29 & 30 BEDFORD STREET, COVENT GARDEN, W.C.
1898

Printed by BALLANTYNE, HANSON & Co.
At the Ballantyne Press

PREFACE

The story of the exploration of the interior of Spitsbergen, begun in 1896, as described in my former book entitled "The First Crossing of Spitsbergen," is continued in the present volume, which is to be regarded as an appendix to that. In 1897 Mr. E. J. Garwood was once more my companion. The illustrations to this book are from photographs taken by him. I here desire to return him my thanks, not only for them, but for many another kindness, for the unbroken good-fellowship of his company, and the stimulus of his society in travel. One of our two Norwegian companions, Nielsen by name, was most serviceable to us. The other was a hindrance. I have called him Svensen in this book, but that was not his name. To render the narrative more complete, I have inserted translations of such published accounts of the expeditions made by Baron Nordenskiöld, his son Gustav Nordenskiöld, and Baron De Geer, as relate to what is vaguely called the "inland ice" of Spitsbergen. I take this opportunity of once more calling attention to the fact that the common spelling "Spitzbergen" is an ignorant blunder; the correct spelling of the name is that employed throughout this book and now adopted in the official publications of the Royal Geographical Society.

CONTENTS

CHAP.		PAGE
I.	KLAAS BILLEN BAY	1
II.	UP THE NORDENSKIÖLD GLACIER	15
III.	BACK TO KLAAS BILLEN BAY	37
IV.	BY WATER TO KINGS BAY	62
V.	THE KING'S HIGHWAY	76
VI.	OSBORNE GLACIER AND PRETENDER PASS	95
VII.	THE SPITSBERGEN DOLOMITES	113
VIII.	RETURN TO KINGS BAY	132
IX.	KINGS BAY TO HORN SOUND	154
X.	ASCENT OF MOUNT HEDGEHOG	170
XI.	ON THE USE OF THE SKI	194
XII.	GEOGRAPHICAL RESULTS	206
	APPENDIX	225

LIST OF ILLUSTRATIONS

Kings Bay Glacier	*Frontispiece*	
The "Expres" in Advent Bay	*facing page*	2
Rough Ice	,,	16
The Colorado Plateau	,,	57
The Head of Kings Bay	,,	71
An Easy Place	,,	80
The Three Crowns from Kings Bay	,,	116
Torrent in a Glacier Ice-foot	,,	161
Horn Sunds Tinder	,,	172
A Ski-fastening	,,	198
A Lapp Shoe	,,	199
New Friesland from Hinlooper Strait	,,	207
Bluffs of the Sassendal	,,	213
Farewell	,,	224

CHAPTER I

KLAAS BILLEN BAY

In the morning of July 9, 1897, Mr. E. J. Garwood and I, along with a small cargo of tourists, were delivered by the steamship *Lofoten* on the shore of Advent Bay, Spitsbergen, just ten days after leaving London. Our party was completed by two men of Vesteraalen, Edward Nielsen and Svensen by name. We had arranged to be met at Advent Bay by the small steamer *Kvik*, which was coming up to cruise about the Spitsbergen coast during the summer. It was annoying to learn that, though she left Tromsö a few days before us, she had not come in. Probably she had been obliged to put back for shelter from the heavy weather. We had no option, therefore, but to pitch our tents and wait.

Companions were not lacking. By our camp sprang up the tents of Herr Ekstam, the Swedish botanist, and of a Norwegian sportsman; further on was a large green tent flying a German flag. There were half-a-dozen hunters' sloops at anchor in the bay, whilst the tourist inn was alive with hurrying men, amongst them Bensen and jovial Peter Hendriksen of the *Fram's* crew. There was plenty for us to do with our baggage, which had all to be unpacked and recombined, some to stay here till we should return for it, the rest to go with us on our first expedition in search of the inland ice. It was a lovely day for this open-air work—a real piece of good-fortune, for nothing is so injurious to baggage as to become well soaked in detail within and without at the very start of a journey. White clouds patched the blue sky and scattered their shadows over the brilliantly green water of Ice Fjord. The snowy ranges beyond were distinct and detailed as though quite near at hand. The air was mild and delightful, and the day was gone before it seemed well begun. Towards evening a gale sprang up and made the tents boom and strain; but we cared not at all, rejoicing rather in the evidence of being once more free from the incumbent protection of walls and roofs.

A wretched morning followed, with drizzle and damp, too painfully reminiscent of last year's weather in the region of bogs. We had nothing to do but to sit inactive and bored, waiting for our steamer which did not come. But, though the *Kvik* was missing, there appeared through the mist our old friend the *Expres*, which last year carried us over a thousand miles round Spitsbergen's coasts and about its bays. She was

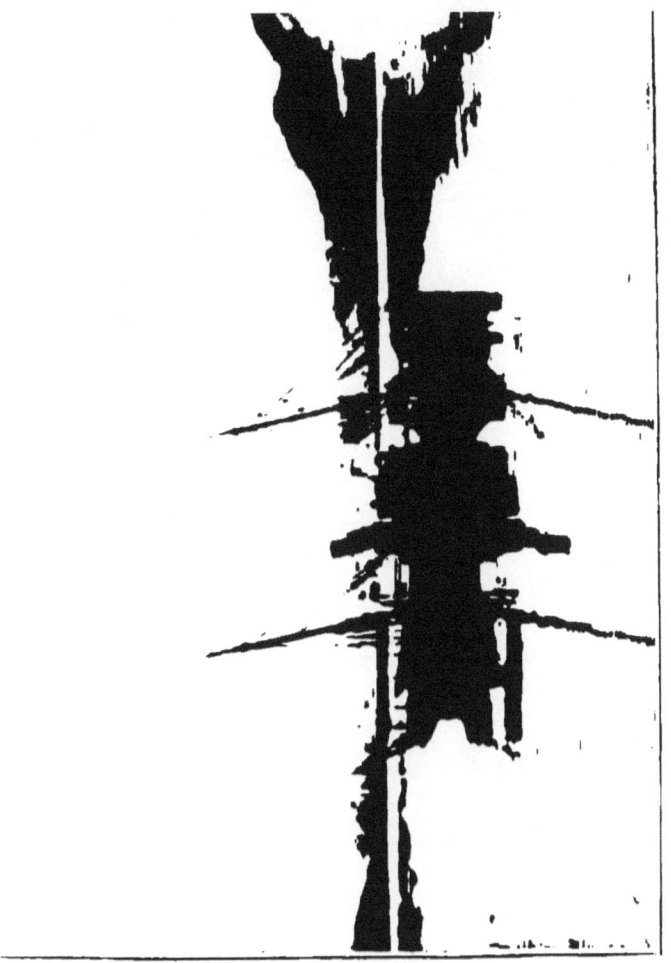

THE "EXPRES" IN ADVENT BAY.

chartered for this season by a German party of sportsmen, Dr. Lerner, Herr G. Meisenbach, and another. They came to see us, and, on hearing of our wretched plight, most kindly offered to take us to Klaas Billen Bay and tow our boat over. We jumped at the chance, and an hour later were comfortably on board, with our men and baggage in our whaleboat behind.

Little more than two hours' steaming brought us to anchor in Skans Bay, a small sheltered inlet cut out of the plateau-mass of Cape Thordsen. We landed at once on the low west shore, where a spit of shingle separates a small lagoon from the bay. Here we left the men to pitch their tent, and set forth inland over the foot of the hillslope. Garwood presently began breaking stones, so I wandered on alone and was soon out of sight. The surroundings would probably strike an unsympathetic eye as dreary. To me they were delightful, though heavy clouds did hang on the tops of the bluffs and all was grey or purple in the solemnity of dim light and utter solitude. Presently came a bold waterfall on the west, where a towering gateway opens upon a secret corrie in the lap of the hills, a place well known to fulmar petrels, who nest hereabouts in great numbers and were swooping to and fro in their bold flight before the cliffs; known, too, to the foxes, to judge by their many tracks. On I tramped over the level valley floor, picking my way amongst boggy places, leaping or wading the channels as they came. All the common arctic flowers were in full bloom, though sparsely scattered about, for this is not one of Spitsbergen's fertile places.

At the head of the bay is a large, flat area, where what once was water is turned to a kind of land. From this flat a series of valleys open, all scooped out from the plateau to which at their heads they rapidly rise. A large valley to the north-east leads over, I suppose, to the Mimesdal; further in is a shorter parallel one with snow at the head. The main valley, however, curved round west of north, and it was this that naturally drew me forward, for in a new country nothing pulls a traveller on so powerfully as a corner round which he cannot see. There lies the unknown with all its possibilities; it is like the fascinating future towards which youth so joyously hastens. Thus I pushed on and on. Round the corner there came into view a glacier filling the valley's head and descending from the high snowy region behind. There was a peak standing further back and looking over at me. The flat valley-floor was a labyrinth of river channels, across which, for the view's sake, I waded, thus reaching a mound of old moraine, on whose top I sat down to survey the melancholy, lonely scene. Birds flying about the cliffs south of the glacier were the only living creatures in sight. There were no reindeer, and not even a footprint or a cast antler. I smoked my pipe in peace and felt once again the charm of utter solitude.

Returning to the bay, I met Garwood, and we went on board the *Expres* together to enjoy the generous hospitality so warmly offered to us by our kind German hosts. Reindeer was cooked, tins opened, corks drawn, and a fine time we had of it for several hours, till at 2 A.M. we dived into our sleeping-bags, Garwood and I lying in the selfsame places where we so often wooed sleep the year before.

Next morning (July 11) the weather was splendid. About 10 o'clock we packed ourselves and our belongings into our whaleboat, bade farewell to our hosts, and rowed off down the calm bay toward Fleur-de-Lys Point, a cape named by the French corvette in 1892. Its base is formed of gypsum, into which the sea eats, so that great fallen masses of the white rock fringe its foot like stranded ice-blocks. A heavy sea was breaking amongst them and tossing towers of spray aloft. We toiled greatly in this broken water and against the wind encountered at the bay's mouth; when the corner was rounded the wind was aft, and we had only the big following seas to trouble us. They rose ominously behind, each in its turn threatening to overwhelm our boat; but, as a matter of fact, little water actually came on board. Thus the noble cliffs of

Skans Bay were left behind, and the deep Klaas Billen Fjord opened ahead. The scenery of it is dull till near its head, the slopes being most barren. We kept up the west side and close in shore, thus gradually finding quieter water.

About two hours up, a little bay tempted us to land for lunch and a hill-scramble; for what can one see from the water-level? It is only when you look down on lake, bay, or ocean that the picturesque value of water is perceived. I suppose I may have climbed five hundred feet or so, Garwood lingering behind to smash rocks. When I turned round on the top of a knoll the view took my breath away. The parallel curving lines of great waves, so big compared with us and our boat, now seemed, with their crests of foam, a mere delicate decoration on the wide surface of the blue bay, upon which the cloud shadows were purple patches. In the barren opposite coast opened a big valley that ran in to a snow mountain in the east. Further round to the left came the splendid Nordenskiöld Glacier, the goal of our present expedition—a splendid river, almost cataract, of ice, sweeping down, in bulging crevassed domes, between fine rock masses from the utterly unknown interior. Its cliff front, rising from the blue water, was fringed with icebergs, some of which, great castellated blocks, floated out by wind and tide, had been passed at the mouth of Skans Bay.

After lunch we rowed on, still hugging the shore, for the seas were big further out, past the mouths of one or two minor valleys leading rapidly up to the snow-field above, and each therefore fitted with its glacier-tongue. Thus the mouth of the wide Mimesdal was reached—a valley interesting to geologists and often visited by previous explorers, though none of them has drawn the vaguest sketch of its plan. We would gladly have spent a day in it, but the water was so shallow at its mouth that we could find no place where the boat could be drawn up; so, as the wind had gone down, we decided to face the loppy, criss-cross sea at once, and camp on the west side of the bay. Our course took us near many icebergs, one a blue tower at least fifty feet out of water. The sea splashed and boomed finely against them.

About a quarter of the way across we opened a full view of a great glacier at the north-west head of Klaas Billen Bay, flowing down a valley approximately parallel to the Mimesdal, between mountains of remarkable form. The peak between it and the Mimesdal, then covered in cloud, we afterwards found to be one of the most striking mountains in this part of Spitsbergen. The Swedes have named it the Pyramid. The glacier leads so far back, and is of so gentle a slope, that, for a moment, we paused to debate whether we should not choose it, rather than Nordenskiöld's Glacier, as an avenue of approach to the interior ; for at that time we were still under the impression that all the glaciers of this region were so many tongues coming down (as do the glaciers of Greenland) from a great inland ice-sheet. Thus the only problem we felt it necessary to consider was, which glacier was the easiest to climb on to and draw our sledges up. Obviously the slope of this glacier was better than that of the Nordenskiöld, whose crevassed nature now became unpleasantly evident. On the other hand, it did not come down to the sea, but poured itself out in the usual low-spreading dome on a wide, alluvial, mud-flat. We had no desire to drag and carry our things over more land than could be helped, so chose the Nordenskiöld Glacier and pulled on.

In a short two hours' rowing we were under the east bank of the bay, where we soon found a quiet cove, and on the shore of it the remains of one of Baron de Geer's camping grounds of last year. There was a place flattened for a tent, there were stones built together for a fire, and there was driftwood collected and cut up for burning—what more could be desired ? The land hereabouts was a large plain stretching a mile or so back to the foot of the hills, whose line of front is carried on by the ice-cliff of the Nordenskiöld Glacier, which thus ends in a little bay of its own. The plain is relatively fertile and should be the home of many reindeer, but all have been

LANDING AT GLACIER'S FOOT

ruthlessly shot out, so that not a hoof-mark did we see, and the only cast antlers were deep in the growing bog. Around this coast are many pools cut off from the bay by ridges of gravel, pushed up by grounded ice when it is pressed against the shore. Here many eider-ducks were feeding, and plenty of skuas, terns, and other birds filled the air with their cries. I walked towards the glacier to find the best way on to it, and was disgusted to discover that between us and the portion of its front that ends on land, and up which we must go, was a considerable stream, flowing in many channels down a stony fan. It was possible at high tide, when a certain submerged moraine was covered, to row round to near the mouth of this stream, but not further, so that we should have to carry all our stuff through the water and over the stones, a distance of perhaps half a mile.

These things we observed because we came to observe them, otherwise our whole attention would have been absorbed by the magnificence of the ice-front of the glacier ending in the sea. We had beheld its full breadth from far away, with the long curdled slopes of ice curving round and coming down to it from the far-away skyline of snow. Now we saw its splintered face in profile from near at hand. How shall I convey the faintest conception of its splendour to a reader who has seen nothing similar? It was not like what I may call the normal arctic glacier, which spreads out at its foot into a very wide, low dome ending all round in an even curve. This glacier is formed by the union of many ice-streams, whose combined volume is wedged together at last between rock walls, and thus broken up by compression. The sea front, therefore, is not a mere cliff, but is the section of a maze of crevasses, and even seracs. There were overhanging towers and enormous caverns, jutting masses and deep holes, all toned in every variety of white and blue and green, shadowed in purple by passing clouds or shining in silver splendour beneath the direct rays of the clear sunlight. The green water was oftenest calm, doubling the vision, which, in some lights, seemed too delicate to be a material reality. Changes of atmospheric clearness and illumination produced infinite varieties of effect, so that the ice-front was never twice the same in appearance. Sometimes it faded away into mist, sometimes it stood out to its remotest end in astonishing clearness of detail. But, under whatever conditions it might be beheld, it was always beautiful, surprising, and rare.

The glacier ends in very shallow water, so that the ice is aground. Very few glaciers in Spitsbergen end in deep water; the one example that occurs to me is the well-known glacier in Cross Bay, which I have only seen from a distance.

GLACIER SNOUTS

For a glacier of given volume and breadth ending in shallow water a definite limit is fixed by the nature of things. A block of ice will float in a depth of water about seven-eighths of its own depth. Thus, the end of a glacier eighty feet thick would be floated away in seventy feet of water, were it not for the cohesion of the mass of the glacier, and the fact that the ice is not reached by the water except on one side, and so does not try to float, but merely forms an embankment to the sea. When the end of the glacier is crevassed the water is enabled to find its way in, to some extent, and thus does something towards lifting partially detached blocks. The snout of a glacier ending in deep water is operated on as a whole by the body of water, and tends to be carried away in very large masses owing to the forward movement of the ice and the leverage of tides. But a glacier ending in shallow water is broken away chiefly by being undermined, to some extent by the mechanical action of the waves, but much more by melting in contact with water often several degrees above the freezing point. When the snout of the glacier is crevassed this undermining effect operates very rapidly. What the depth of water actually is below the foot of the cliff we were unable to determine; I do not think that it is more than ten feet at low tide, the height of the cliff being from eighty to one hundred feet. It must be borne in mind that the glacier brings down a considerable quantity of moraine, most of which is dumped into the water just at the foot of the cliff. Thus the depth is constantly being filled up, and if the process went forward without any countervailing action the ice-cliff would be cut off from the sea by a wall of moraine within a very short time. That it is not so cut off is partly due to the denuding action of the waves, but more to the fact that, when the depth is diminished to a certain definite level, the glacier must advance over the newly-formed soil, and so the process is continued. Thus, every glacier ending in a cliff in shallow water must be advancing. As soon as it ceases to advance it must deposit a moraine embankment round its base, cutting itself off from the water. When this has happened the cliff ceases to exist; a terminal slope takes its place. Streams of water flowing from it cut down and distribute the moraine. The water then continues to be invaded by a débris fan, formed of alluvial matter in the ordinary way. The glacier previously mentioned, which is at the north-west corner of Klaas Billen Bay, is an example of a glacier which, doubtless, once ended in the fjord, but has been lifted up and cut off from the water by moraine materials brought down by itself.

It was as delightful as it was interesting to sit and watch the noble glacier-front, in all the wealth of its colouring and the wonder of

CALVING OF THE GLACIER 13

its form. At high and low tide the ice was stable, and hardly any falls took place; but at other times falls were frequent, most frequent towards half-tide. Then the ice-cliff fired great guns along all its battlemented front in rapid succession. At moments of good luck one chanced to be looking just where the fall took place. Sometimes a great tower would slowly bend over; at other times its base would crush together, and it would start sliding vertically. In either case, before it had moved far it would be intersplit and riven into smaller masses, which, falling together with a sound like thunder, would ding and splash up the water into a tower of spray, a hundred feet high perhaps. Then, if they fell in a deep place, the ice-blocks would heave and roll about for a while, lifting the water upon their sides and shaking it off in cataracts, till at last they came to rest, or went slowly floating away amongst countless fellows gone before. Meanwhile the circling waves started by the fall would be spreading around, washing up against the multitude of floating blocks in the bay, disturbing the equilibrium of some and toppling them over or splitting them up, thus starting new rings of waves. At last the great waves would come swishing along the shore, louder and louder as they approached, till they broke close by the tent, and washed up to where our whaleboat was lying, hauled just beyond their reach. Between whiles was heard only the ceaseless murmur of the bay and the gentle soughing of the wind.

At high tide we rowed our boat round as near to the foot of the glacier as we dared go, and pitched our final camp by the stream already mentioned. It was nearly a mile from the foot of the easiest line of approach up the moraine on to the surface of the glacier. We hauled our heavy boat up high and dry with great toil, assembled in our larger tent the baggage we were going to leave behind, arranged the loads for our two sledges, and, in repeated journeys, laboriously dragged and carried them over bog and stones to the foot of the steep moraine, greatly disturbing the minds of a number of terns, who had their nests on the stony ground near the channels of the river. They swooped almost on to our heads, and hovered, screaming frightfully, not more than a yard out of reach. No bird that flies has a more frail or graceful appearance than a tern. When the sun shines on them as they hover amongst the floating ice-blocks they seem the very incarnation of whatsoever is purest, gentlest, and most fair. But there is in every tern the pugnacity of a bargee and the fractiousness of seven swearing fishwives. They are everlastingly at war with the skuas and the kittiwakes, and they always seem to come off best in an encounter. We, at any rate, were not sorry to quit their ground and leave them glorying over our retreat.

CHAPTER II

UP THE NORDENSKIÖLD GLACIER

OUR preparations being completed, we set forth up the Nordenskiöld Glacier, toward the unknown interior, on the morning of July 13. The first struggle up the steep, moraine-faced front of the glacier involved all our forces. The stones, lying upon ice, were loose and large. They slipped from under, or fell upon us. We took one sledge at a time and lightened it of half its burden, but still it was hard to drag. It wedged itself against rocks when pulled forward, but never seemed to find a stone to stop its backsliding. Our aim was to reach a tongue of hard snow in the upper part of a gully. Coming to it from the side, the sledge swung across and almost upset us all. At last we reached the top, returned for the second sledge, then (two or three times) for the bundles, and so finally gained our end after hours of toil. Once on more level ice, things went better, though not well. To begin with, the sledges were badly loaded and had to be rearranged. Then, though the surface of the ice sloped but

16 UP THE NORDENSKIÖLD GLACIER

gently, it was very lumpy and the lumps turned the sledges this way and that. Garwood and I pulled one, the two men the other. Perspiration ran off us. Our estimate of the possible length of the day's march diminished.

Nordenskiöld Glacier, as has been said, descends in a great curve. It comes down from the north and ends flowing west. It receives two large tributaries from the east. If we had kept right round the immense sweep of the glacier's left bank, we should have avoided a peck of troubles, but must have travelled miles out of the way, for our destination was northward. As it was, we steered a middle course, and thereby came into a most unsafe tangle of crevasses. The step-like descent of the ice prevented seeing far ahead. We were constantly in hope that the next plateau would be smooth, but each as it came was crevassed like its predecessor, whilst the slopes between were almost impassable. Any one who knows the Gorner Glacier, below the Riffelhorn, will be able to picture this part of the Nordenskiöld Glacier. It was almost as badly broken up as that. To drag sledges up such a place is no simple job. Most of the crevasses were half full of rotten winter snow, but it was only by bridges of this unreliable substance that they could be crossed at all. Ultimately we found ourselves in a *cul-de-sac*, cut off ahead, to right, and to left by huge impassable

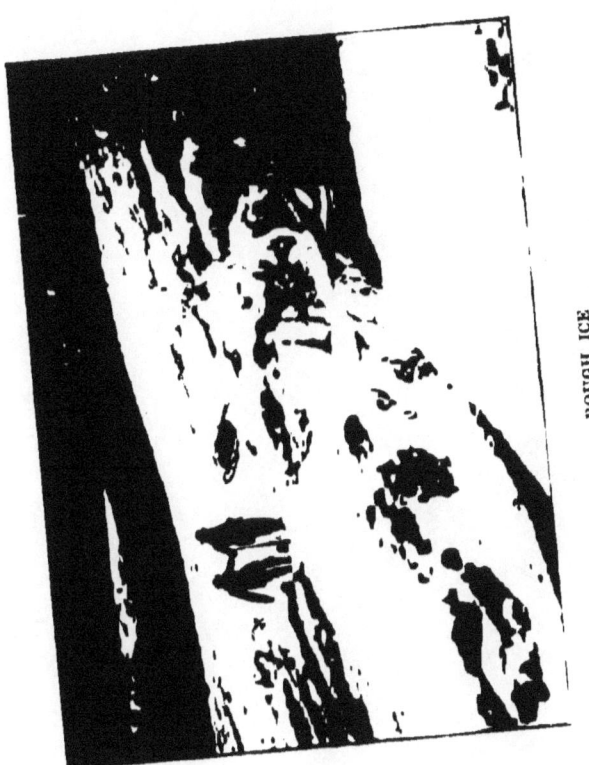

ROUGH ICE

schrunds. There was nothing for it but to go back a distance that had been won by more than an hour's toil. We left the sledges lying, and scattered to prospect. A way was eventually discovered whereby, when every one was fairly worn out, the worst part of the ascent was completed. After crossing the last big crevasse, it was agreed that enough had been done. Camp was pitched about 700 feet above the level of the bay.

Now only had we leisure to look about and drink in the fine quality of the scenery; not that a man is blind to scenery when engaged in toilsome physical exertion, but he is incapable of analysing it or noticing its more delicate and evanescent qualities. For this reason I maintain that the observers in explorations should be freed as much as possible from the mere mechanical labour of making the way. Every foot-pound of energy put into sledge-hauling, for instance, precludes more important mental activities. This was not Garwood's opinion at the beginning of our journey, but he came round to my way of thinking before the end. From the level of our camp we looked down the whole riven slope o the glacier to the broad blue bay below, dotted all over with floating ice and flashing eyes of light from the hidden sun. Farther away came the bleak recesses of the Mimesdal, and a range of snow mountains to the right. There was a level

18 UP THE NORDENSKIÖLD GLACIER

roof of cloud at an altitude of about 1000 feet, casting on the hills that richness of purple tone so characteristic of Spitsbergen's dull days. Most beautiful was the glacier-cascade, and especially the immediate foreground of crevasses, on to, or rather into, which we looked down and beheld the splendid colour of their walls. They are far bluer than Alpine crevasses, almost purple indeed, in their depths. Here, of course, on the broken ice were no streams, though below the crevasses there had been so many that the air was filled with their tinkling, whilst the deep bass of *moulins* was continually heard. Ahead came the clouds, into which the glacier disappeared, the last outlines visible being low white domes of the usual arctic sort. It was pleasant to sit in the still, cool air while ice-lumps were melting and other preparations making for supper. "Look! look!" cried Nielsen, "there is a bird as white as snow." It was an ivory gull come to inspect us. The only other visitors were fulmar petrels, whose nesting-place on the cliffs of the Terrier we were to discover a few days later.

Our camp consisted of two small tents, one an old Mummery tent of Willesden drill, the other six inches larger in all directions, and made of a slightly stronger canvas. Both tents had floors of the same material sewn in—an excellent arrangement, rendering them perfectly safe in any gale that blew. They served us well throughout

HONEYCOMB ICE

the summer, and are still in almost as good condition as when they came from Edgington's hands. Long I sat in silence and alone, watching the opalescent bay with its ever-varying colours and floating icebergs, the purple hills striped and capped with snow, the wide, deeply-penetrating, mysterious valleys, the great icefield sloping down in front, and the frame of cloud arching in the whole. The crunching of snow and ice by human feet and the sound of voices showed that the others were returning from their ramble, hungry and with good news, as it proved, for the way was open ahead.

Next morning (14th) we pursued our onward journey, still struggling through crevasses for about an hour, then finding a fairly even though none too gentle slope, up which it was possible to advance steadily. So far the hard ice of the glacier had formed the surface. It gradually became less and less firm, and turned into a kind of icy honeycomb, built of a granular fabric that crushed together ankle-deep under the foot. The cells of this honeycomb ice were of all sizes, some as big as a lead-pencil, others large enough to hold the foot, others again to fall into bodily. Each cell was more or less filled with water, whilst the top was often disguised by a lid of ice with a little snow on it, so that the existence of the water-hole was not suspected till one trod through into the freezing puddle. We came to understand what to look out for, at this level of Spitsbergen glaciers, and to walk warily; but at first we plunged and stumbled about in the most annoying fashion, becoming very wet, cold, and out of temper. Further up, the snow covering was more continuous, till, at a level of about 1000 feet above the sea, we were no longer walking upon ice, but upon frozen snow. In fact, here was true *névé*, the like of which our last year's experiences had led us to believe did not exist in Spitsbergen.

This is only one of many differences observed between the strangely temperate region south of Ice Fjord, explored by us in 1896, and the region north of Ice Fjord, and so close to it, explored in 1897. The former is to be described as sub-arctic, the latter is truly arctic in every sense. The Sassendal region is a land of bogs and disintegrating hillsides, with cataracts and many waters. The Klaas Billen and King's Bay area is ice-covered at levels which are ice-free so few miles away. The causes of this great contrast are obscure.

All too soon the cloud-roof descended upon us, or rather we ascended into it. Rain began to fall. The snow being soft and the slope continuing steep, our work waxed laborious again, and so continued. We steered, by compass, a little east of north, the direction of the east foot of the group of mountains against which the glacier, in bending round, leans its right bank. The highest of these was known to us as De Geer Peak, because it was ascended by De Geer in 1882. In the thickening fog our men began to betray unwillingness to proceed. They mistrusted us and our compass. At sea, they said, a man could steer by compass, but this was not sea, and they had never heard of going overland after a magnetic needle. Four hours' marching preceded a halt for lunch in the midst of the undulating white desert, which stretched away on all sides into clouds. Not far off was a blue lake, like a sapphire set in silver—a lovely object, and the only thing clearly visible except a single crevasse and the ghosts of the bases of the mountains. At times the clouds parted a little, and then we could discover a seafog creeping up from below. In the gap between it and the lower level of the clouds was a far-off glimpse of Ice Fjord, with the hills of Advent Bay beyond.

When fog and clouds joined we set forward again, and worked on steadily uphill. The snow grew softer and softer. We fastened one sledge behind the other, and harnessed ourselves all four to the front one, but the change profited little. Hour now succeeded hour, and nothing came in sight. The only variation was in the degree of slope. Every few minutes we stopped to observe the compass, and always found that we had bent away to left or right of the proper track; sometimes we were even going at right angles to it.

When all were tired, we pitched camp on a flat place, which we thought might prove to be the plateau at the foot of De Geer Peak. The tents were set up with some difficulty, in a fluster of wind, upon the soft snow, and moored ahead and astern to the two sledges, the site being about 1500 feet above sea-level. The temperature was a few degrees below freezing. The oil-stove burning in the tent was a comforting companion, though we changed our opinion about it when the steam from the pot condensed on the roof and fell in rain all over our things.

All night long the wind howled, the clouds grew denser, and snow fell with increasing heaviness. When we looked forth in the morning nothing was visible, beyond our camp, in any direction. The tents and sledges were almost snowed under. As we had no notion in what direction to bend our steps, nor what any part of the interior might be like, it was necessary to wait for a clearance; so we lay in our sleeping-bags, cooked, played dominoes with numbered scraps of paper, and otherwise killed time. The men, I fear, were pretty miserable, for the expedition had no interest to them and they were full of all sorts of vain terrors. They confessed that for fear of bears they had been unable to sleep! They hourly expected to be buried under some avalanche of snow or to fall into some hidden pit. Nielsen soon got over his terrors, but they increased upon

Svensen to our no small discomfort. As Nielsen said: "Svensen has never been away from his old woman before. He is accustomed to go fishing in the morning, and then to come home for his dinner. He isn't used to the kind of food that you give him, and he isn't used to this sort of place." The more we knew of Nielsen the better we liked him. He talked excellent English, with a smack of the sea in every phrase. He was always on the alert to be helpful, and had plenty of conversation and some good stories. Svensen knew no English, except a few seamen's phrases. He was a good enough fellow, but he hated his novel surroundings, and was only counting the days till he should reach his home again.

Not till 7 o'clock in the evening did the fog lift, and then it disclosed no very distant view. Close at hand were the rocks at the foot of De Geer Peak; we were encamped at the exact point we had meant to reach—a small plateau or shelf of snow on the glacier's extreme right margin, just where the rock slope of the mountain begins. In all other directions the white *névé* went undulating away, trending in the main uphill to north and east, downhill to the south. There was no definite object in sight when we turned our backs to the tent and the crags; elsewhere vaguely outlined clouds drifted about, brushing the snow with apparent aimlessness. It was a view composed of different tones of white. Ice-blink filled the air. It was impossible to estimate distances with the smallest degree of accuracy. Looking out of the tent-door, I saw what I thought was a bear moving along—most improbable of beasts at such an altitude. I was in dread lest the men should see it, and become yet more unwilling to face the lonely interior. A moment later the light changed, and the bear was revealed as a bit of waste paper fluttering along in the breeze. In a few minutes the fog came down again, not very densely. Garwood and I were for starting on at once, but the men considered that it was time for supper, with bed to follow. On the whole we decided to let them have their wish, and to use the hours for trying the *ski*.

Ski (pronounced *shee*) are the snowshoes of Norway and Sweden, which Nansen's books have been chiefly instrumental in making known to Englishmen. They may be described as thin boards, six feet or more long, and about five inches wide, curved up and brought to a point in front (like the shoes of a fifteenth-century dude), and cut off square behind. Nansen has told how the Scandinavians are accustomed to the use of them from childhood up, what facility they attain, and the wonderful feats they become able to perform with them. We were concerned to discover how far an untaught Englishman could use them at all, and how long was needed for learning to get about on them. We were entirely ignorant about them, so that we started with every disadvantage. To begin with, there are all sorts and kinds of ski—long and narrow, short and broad, polished and unpolished, grooved below in different ways, attachable to the foot by different systems, made of different sorts and kinds of wood. Of all this we knew nothing. We went into the first shop we saw in Bergen and bought the first pair of ski that were offered to us, with a loop arrangement of cane covered with leather to attach them to the feet. As it turned out our choice was pretty lucky. I shall hereafter devote a chapter to ski, so more need not be said about them in this place.

With great deliberation, and after many blunders, we inserted our feet into the loops, one loop or wide strap going firmly over the toe, the other passing round the heel, so that the foot can be easily bent and that when it is turned to right or left the ski turns with it. Then we gingerly straightened ourselves up and prepared to shuffle away, each clutching an ice-axe for a third leg. It became immediately apparent that our plateau was not quite flat, for we began to slide downhill. Our legs separated from one another and over we fell. It is easier to fall down than to get up again. Our feet were twisted out of the loops and had to be brought back into place. Endeavouring to arrange matters, I loosened one of my ski, and off it started on its own account downhill.

I saw it disappear into the fog, and sent Svensen after it. He was gone half an hour or more, and came back shuffling on it. Then I tried again, this time uphill.

The first thing to do was to turn round. Of course I trod with one ski on the top of the other, and tumbled over again. When one paid attention to the forward halves of the ski the hind halves got mixed, and *vice versâ*. Uphill, however, we advanced well enough, as long as there was a crust of snow to go upon, but where the ice was blown bare by the wind we slid about helplessly, for the boards do not bite like skates. Of course on such places ski are seldom needed, the crust of ice being usually strong enough to support the foot. Having reached the foot of the rocks we tried sliding down. After two or three attempts we found our balance; the process is similar to a standing glissade, only that the motion is quicker. Any good glissader can soon learn to slide down a moderately steep slope on ski. When the snow is uneven, still more when it is of varying textures (soft in one place, slippery in another), new difficulties of balancing arise. After an hour's practice we found our feet well enough, and were assured of being able to cover the ground at a reasonable rate.

Next we tried the Canadian snowshoes, and found them easy enough to work, but very clumsy compared with the ski. We afterwards learnt that

ASCENT OF DE GEER PEAK   27

our principal trouble with the latter was caused by the unsuitability of our footgear. We had been told to wear large fur boots of the kind called Finnsku, with hay packed in them. They may be well enough if you know how to pack them, and if they are of the right dimensions. Ours were wrong every way. It was only when we gave them up and took to our ordinary Swiss climbing-boots that we became really comfortable as well as firm on our feet. To this important question of footgear reference will also be made hereafter.

If the weather had been fine, or the least chance of a view could have been discerned, we should have delayed to repeat the ascent of De Geer Peak. Luck, however, was against us. As De Geer's account of his climb is buried, for English readers, in a Swedish scientific publication,* a translation of it is here inserted:

"On the morning of August 2, 1882, I set forth from the coast, in company with Lund and the ship's boy, on an expedition up the little valley bordering the north side of Nordenskiöld Glacier. The bottom of this valley, with its small hills and little lakes, resembled some unwooded tract of Sweden. . . . Arrived at the head of the valley, we put on the rope and struck across the first side glacier. We had now reached the inland ice and were about 600 metres above sea-level. As there was no time for a long

* K. Vetenskaps Akad. Hand. Bihang, ix., No. 2, p. 46.

28 UP THE NORDENSKIÖLD GLACIER

expedition over the ice, we decided to climb the mountain near at hand. The only plants found on its slope were some mosses and lichens. Of birds we only saw one fulmar petrel, which came flying over the inland ice. The top of the mountain was covered with old hard-packed snow. Its altitude according to the barometer was over 1200 metres above the sea. It is therefore, after Hornsunds Tind, the highest mountain hitherto measured in Spitsbergen, though there appear to be other mountains in its neighbourhood at least as high.

"The view was remarkably comprehensive. In the south-west was a long stretch of Ice Fjord's south coast. In clear weather it would probably have been possible to see both the mouth of the fjord and Mount Nordenskiöld, the high mountain west of Advent Bay which Nathorst afterwards climbed. We had an uninterrupted view over a great part of the broken hill-country west of Klaas Billen Bay, which appears to be devoid of big glaciers. Eastward the inland ice stretched away from the foot of the mountain, spreading out its gently undulating surface away to a remote mountain group, situated between N. $69\frac{1}{2}°$ E. and N. $101°$ E., probably identical with the range marked on the map ending westward in Mount Edlund, near Wybe Jans Water. Yet further away appeared a sunlit streak, and beyond that again a line of mountains, certainly very remote. These were quite clear and distinct for a long time till clouds covered them up. Perhaps they lie along the west coast of Barents Land. . . . In the north-east the interior of the ice was covered with clouds, so that Mount Chydenius could not be seen, which otherwise would probably have been visible. Most striking was the view to the north-west, in which direction we recognised, on first arriving at the top, a large piece of water, doubtless the West Fjord of Wijde Bay. Its innermost part lay in the direction between N. 39° W. and N. 27½° W., and was only hidden for a short distance by a mountain (the compass deviation is assumed to have been N. 14° W.).* Between us and Wijde Bay no mountains were seen, but only big, apparently level glaciers, filling the bottom of the great valley and seeming to form an ice-divide. It is worth mention that no ice was seen in the blue waters of Wijde Bay, although unbroken sea-ice is reported to have invested at least the western part of Spitsbergen's north coast throughout the whole summer.

"When we first arrived on the top I took some photo-

---

* This is doubtless the direction of West Fjord of Wijde Bay, but it seems doubtful whether any considerable proportion of it can be visible from the summit of De Geer's Peak. All along the south-east side of West Fjord lies a continuous range of hills, a photograph of which is now before me. The lowest point of this range between Cape Petermann and Mount Sir Thomas at the head of the fjord can scarcely be as low as 500 feet, whilst almost the whole of the range is 1000 feet high. The average width of the fjord is about two miles, but just at one point it is five miles wide. The height of De Geer's Peak is given as over 1200 metres, say 4000 feet. Its distance from West Fjord is about thirty geographical miles. If the intervening hill range happens to sink below the level of about 600 feet, exactly in the line of sight to the place where the fjord is five miles wide, the extreme edge of the water would just be visible; yet, even then, no considerable body of water could be seen. But De Geer states that there were no hills between the fjord and his peak. Is it not possible that what he saw was the East Fjord, at whose head are no mountains? Some undetected iron in the rock on which he stood might be responsible for the compass deviation. The rocks of Spitsbergen are full of such surprises.

graphs and observed a number of angles, besides making some sketches, but little by little our peak became enveloped in clouds which swept over from the inland ice. We waited four hours on the top, hoping it would clear, but the weather only became thicker and a wind sprang up, so that we were compelled to begin the descent. We followed the south-west ridge, which is certainly the best route for the ascent, in case this point of view should be revisited as a station of the proposed meridian-arc measurement. The return to the tent was made by the afore-mentioned valley."

From this description it appears that the part of the country we intended to traverse was hidden from De Geer by clouds. We had no information whatever, therefore, as to the lie of the land or the direction in which we should steer. Next morning was somewhat clearer. The Terrier range on the further side of the glacier was disclosed, as well as some snowy domes inland, apparently very remote, but really not far off. The glacier was perceived to trend back in a direction somewhat east of north, and to widen out greatly. It seemed as though this were a true sheet of inland ice of the Greenland sort. We set forward hopefully in a clear interval, so laying our course as to keep up the glacier's right side.

During the first hour Garwood's snowshoes gave him great trouble, for he had chosen the Canadian pair. When he had changed them with Nielsen for ski, of which unfortunately

FOG ON THE SNOWFIELD

we had only three pairs with us, and after a series of halts for readjustments, we got fairly under way. It was a steady uphill pull for about three hours. The fog soon came down, denser than ever, and lasted the rest of the day. Only by the resistance of the sledges could the steepness of the slope be inferred. There was absolutely nothing to be seen. It is hard for any one who has not experienced it to conceive the absolute invisibility of everything in the rather dazzling light that pervades a fog upon snow. The effect is thus described by Mr. Peary, writing about Greenland :[*]

"Not only was there no object to be seen, but in the entire sphere of vision there was no difference in intensity of light. My feet and snowshoes were sharp and clear as silhouettes, and I was sensible of contact with the snow at every step. Yet, as far as my eyes gave me evidence to the contrary, I was walking upon nothing. The space between my snowshoes was as light as the zenith. The opaque light which filled the sphere of vision might come from below as well as above. A curious mental as well as physical strain resulted from this blindness with wide-open eyes, and sometimes we were obliged to stop and await a change."

Of course, in such a vague illumination there are no shadows. The light comes equally from everywhere. To keep a straight course requires

[*] "My Arctic Journal," London, 1894, p. 232.

32 UP THE NORDENSKIÖLD GLACIER

continual attention. The compass must be referred to continually.

When the sledges felt heavier we knew that the slope steepened. About three miles, as we guessed, from camp, they suddenly took a plunge forward on their own account and were with difficulty restrained. We had crossed a watershed, and the slope was downhill. One sledge knocked Svensen off his feet and sent his ski flying. He captured the right, but the left vanished hissing into the fog. He followed it, and became utterly invisible a few yards away. While we awaited his return, a ghostly sun appeared for a moment, but was swallowed up again. Absolute silence reigned. The air was motionless. We could just see one another, and that was all. At the foot of the hill came a level area, then uphill again, steeper than before. Fortunately for us novices on ski the snow was not in a slippery condition. On the contrary, it tended to adhere to the ski, so that they held the ground well without backsliding. It was deep, soft snow, into which we should have sunk at least to the knee had we been merely walking in boots. As it was, we did not sink into it at all, and could drag the sledges with our full weight. Nielsen was the only miserable one of the party, for he had the Canadian snowshoes. His feet kept slipping out of the straps when he strained upon them in pulling. Moreover, he could not accustom himself to keep his legs wide enough apart, and so was always tripping up or treading with one shoe on the other. All day the cold was considerable, the air full of frozen vapour which incrusted us over, so that heads, hair, and clothes became a mass of icicles tinkling as we walked. After making about seven miles, chiefly uphill, we camped at a height of some 2500 feet. It was pleasant to feel the shelter of the tents, pleasanter still to get the stove going and gain a drink of water to slake the parching thirst from which all were suffering.

Early next morning (17th) the clouds broke for a brief interval, as they have a way of doing about 6 A.M., even in the worst weather. Looking back we saw the watershed crossed the previous day, and learnt that we had (unnecessarily) descended into the head of a big valley trending west, that we had crossed this and reascended its northern side to the place of encampment. Had we been able to see ahead, both the descent and the reascent might have been avoided. De Geer Peak was in sight to the south; westward, as we looked down the valley, a single, or perhaps a double, row of hills intervened between us and Dickson Bay. They were all white with permanent snow. Not a patch of open country was visible there. One of these hills, apparently the Lyktan, was capped with a limestone crown. In the silence and stillness of the cold morning these mountains, for all their relative littleness, looked singularly dignified. They were so grey and shaggy, creatures of storm and everlasting winter, things utterly remote from all association with man, even as the very mountains of the moon. While we were watching them, clouds came up again in the lap of the south-west wind. The milky fog settled down before we started on, and nothing more was seen that day.

Svensen began to complain of feeling unwell, talked of pains in his inside, of numbness in feet and legs, and so forth. For the matter of that, no one felt particularly bright, the process of coming into condition being always laborious. The only thing to be done was to push on. It was uphill all the time, often up slopes so steep that one sledge had to be left while all four concentrated their efforts on raising the other. Now and then the slope bent away down to the west, showing that we were keeping close along the watershed. The course taken was a little east of north. The work was harder than ever. Hour after hour passed, and yet the hoped-for high plateau was not found. Snow fell heavily and the wind became violent. It had its compensations, however, for we could steer by it. The fresh snow was unsuited for ski. It froze on beneath them and balled, an impediment to the shuffling action of the feet.

As the fresh snow accumulated, the surface of the old snow beneath became so hard that ultimately ski could be discarded. A final long tug up a very steep slope completed the morning's march. At the top Svensen threw himself down and said he could go no further. He certainly looked ill. His face was ghastly grey, his cheeks sunken, his eyes staring out of his head and blood-shot. The storm was raging furiously, driving the fresh snow along, like a waist-deep stream of opaque white fluid, with a loud hissing noise that mingled in the roar of the wind. It was decided to pitch one of the tents and take shelter in it, while a hot lunch was cooked; but to carry out the plan was not easy in the teeth of the gale. When the tent was at last set up, Svensen was pushed in and the rest of us crowded after. The sick man began to tremble all over and moaned horribly. He pitied himself in broken accents. There was nothing for it but to pitch the second tent, unpack his fur sleeping-bag and stow him away to warm up. While this was being done I rubbed him hard all over to restore circulation.

Before we had been halted half an hour tents and sledges were almost buried beneath the drifting snow. The gale was getting worse every minute, making the roofs boom and flap so that we feared they would rip asunder. Meanwhile cooking went forward, and then all slept, awaiting a change of weather. Late in the evening there was no improvement, and Svensen said he was going to die. By morning the wind had dropped, but the fog was yet denser. The sledges were not to be seen. The tents were hidden from one another behind walls and heaps of drifted snow. Nielsen shouted that Svensen was "all broken up," and could not be moved. I went to see him, and found a miserable-looking object. He said he had swellings in his middle and talked about an old sprain and the cold. His legs were senseless below the knees. Here was a pretty mess, if his story were true! We had suspicions that fright was a large factor in his trouble; but if it were not, and we made the man go on, what a responsibility would lie upon us! He was emphatic that he could not stir a yard that day, and that if we insisted on his moving we must carry him, son of Anak that he was. There still remained food for six days, so we could afford to wait twenty-four hours at any rate. Practically we had no option.

CHAPTER III

BACK TO KLAAS BILLEN BAY

GARWOOD and I, for exercise, started out on ski, not daring to go far in the dense fog, for, except by following up the track, it was impossible to find the camp again once it had passed out of sight. With the surface snow in such feathery condition, a track would be obliterated in two minutes, even by a light wind. Caution, therefore, was essential. The calm continuing, we indulged in longer excursions, trudging always uphill, and sliding down again with increasing confidence and ease. Assuredly, for the mere movement, ski-glissading is first-rate fun. Taking a longer range uphill than before, we came into a thinner patch of fog, with a quarter-mile reach of vision, perhaps, and the white ghost of a sun aloft. Something suggested that a domed hilltop was close ahead. We pushed on, and rose above the fog. Clear was the atmosphere in all directions below a roof of cloud, white and level, the far-extending floor of fog through which we had just emerged, as through a trapdoor on to the stage. In front (to the east), and on our left (to the north), gentle snow-slopes rose to skylines seemingly near at hand. We could not but push on. The snow was in perfect condition for sliding, the air delightfully crisp. It was grateful merely to have left the clammy fog behind. The convex curve of the snowfield was cause of the constant retreat of the skyline from our advance; but at last a distant summit peeped over, then another. Evidently there was a watershed, and from it a view. It developed very slowly, but at length it was all there—a downhill slope in front, and then the distance filled with a prospect on which no human eye had ever gazed. It was strictly an eastward view, for in the north the snowfield rose higher, and to the south fog enveloped everything.

Whether it was the effect of contrast after the blindness of three days, or whether the view was absolutely superb, is hard to say; it certainly impressed us as a very grand sight. We were standing at the head of a broad snow-white valley, to which a long slope drooped from our feet, the level of the valley-floor being at least 1000 feet below us, or more than 2000 feet above sea-level. On either side the valley was enclosed by faces of rock, bluff-fronts cut out of what was formerly a big plateau, level with our position. A splintered nunatak pierced through the glacier below and formed an

MOUNT CHYDENIUS

effective centre-piece. The glacier itself swept away in its wide, dignified fashion, first east, then gradually round in a great curve to the south-east, on its slow crawl towards Wybe Jans Water. The row of bluffs on the left (north) were seen, one beyond another, stretching away fainter and fainter to the remote distance, where the last may look down upon the east coast. The nearest and highest of these bluffs appears to be the Mount Chydenius of Nordenskiöld. Further north and masked by clouds were indications of a range of peaks of bolder form.

We returned to camp for our cameras and came back with Nielsen, then Garwood set forward down the hill to investigate the Hecla Hook rocks of the nunatak, whilst Nielsen and I went north up the snow-slope. We had not more than a mile to go before reaching the top of the highest snow-dome in the watershed area between the glacier systems draining west to Dickson Bay, south-east to Wybe Jans Water, and south to Klaas Billen Bay. Whether the glacier to the north bent ultimately west to Dickson Bay or round to the head of East Fjord of Wijde Bay could not be determined, for it was soon lost beneath a roof of cloud. The fulmar petrels that came flying over could have told us. The range of hills across the north was now clear. There were indications of a valley between our plateau and them, and of a pass leading over to it from a bay of the eastern valley. Unfortunately my photographs of this important view, like all others taken by me on roller film this year, failed. How I now regret not to have carried some good glass plates to this point! Only blind notes remain. There was a peak of nearly 4000 feet, 30° west of north, and another due north about six miles away. Connected with them were many more of smaller dimensions. West of the peak first mentioned the land dropped below the cloud-level, which was from 500 to a 1000 feet beneath our feet. All in the Dickson Bay direction was hidden under piled masses of cloud.

It was a fascinating and tantalising view. One more day's march would have solved for certain, instead of merely by inference, the whole question of the topography of this icy area. Any one of the peaks ahead would have commanded views towards Wijde Bay, Hinloopen Strait, and Wybe Jans Water. But with Svensen *hors de combat* we were helpless. To leave camp for a whole day was impossible, seeing that, in this featureless white wilderness, if fog came on, we should never find it again, whilst, without us, the men left behind could not steer their way to the coast. I thought, however, that it might be possible to return by a new route, descending first down the east valley and then working round to the south; so we went back to the tents and asked Svensen whether, if we dragged his sledge, he could follow on his own feet homeward. He eagerly jumped at the suggestion; the stuff was packed and off we started uphill to the point of our first view at the head of the east valley. Svensen shuffled along on his ski well enough, though with a sorry countenance. When he found us going uphill he protested that that could not be the way back and that we were going east instead of south. Arrived at the top and seeing the valley he became mutinous, said if we went down there we should all leave our bones in this horrible land, and generally protested with all his might. Nielsen joined his protests, on the ground that, Svensen being the sort of man he was and apparently ill as well as terrified, we should probably soon find ourselves obliged to drag him along on a sledge, and that, while he could manage to walk, it was best to get him in the direction of the coast, so that, if ultimately he had to be carried, it might be over as few miles as possible. In fact, we were cornered; there was nothing for it but to turn coastward.

Before doing so we took one more long gaze over the great glacier and away to the remote hills that look down on Wybe Jans Water. One of them must be Mount Edlund, another the White Mountain near Heley's Sound; but it was impossible to identify them. These were the peaks climbed by Nordenskiöld and his party in

1864. As they were the only people who have ever gazed inland over this same sea of ice, I here insert an abbreviated translation of their account.*

"On August 21, 1864, the weather became so fine that we returned to land in order to climb Mount Edlund. We landed at the edge of the glacier, which ends without a cliff. Parallel with the shore, at a distance of about a thousand yards, there extends a broad bank of moraine, beyond which comes the glacier itself. Its lowest part consists of a mounded ice-field, here and there split by crevasses, for the most part filled with water. The ascent was easy, and we soon reached the lowest plateau of the mountain. A grass-slope followed, becoming steeper higher up and ending near the upper plateau in a hyperite cliff faced by four-edged columns. This cliff was at least fifty feet high, and vertical; but the rocks were firm, and could easily be climbed. Thus we reached the top.

"'The view fully came up to our expectations. Northwestward, far as the eye could reach, spread endless hills and plains of snow, only broken here and there by occasional mountain peaks standing more or less free. Among these, several remote mountains, probably surrounding the southern shore of Wijde Bay, deserve mention. Further round in the north-east a row of

---

* "Die Schwedischen Expeditionen nach Spitzbergen und Bären-Eiland ausgeführt in den Jahren 1861, 1864, and 1868 unter Leitung von O. Torell und A. E. Nordenskiöld. Aus dem Schwedischen übersetzt von L. Passarge." Jena, 1869. 8vo, pp. 470 *et seq.*

peaks stood up against the horizon. Mount Chydenius was the most northerly and highest of these great mountains.* We overlooked the whole of Wybe Jans Water from Whale's Point and Whale's Head to its inmost recess near the White Mountain. Many mountains surrounded by ice reared themselves in the west. The view over Hinloopen Strait was hindered by thick mist, which appeared to lie only over this depression and its bordering hills, as so often happens.

"In order to follow up the mountain ridge extending towards the north-west, and to learn whether an expedition over the snow fields involved difficulties, we went from the summit farther into the interior of the land, which lay almost at the same height as the peak. It was quite level and covered with hard, frozen snow, on which walking was as easy as on a floor. This plain of snow appeared to stretch away to Mount Chydenius, so that that peak would be easy to reach for the purposes of a triangulation. We went as far as a distant small hill of snow [apparently the Mount Svanberg of the map] without any new experiences, except that fresh peaks kept constantly appearing above the snow; we accordingly decided to return.

"The shortest way back to the ship led down a rather steep ice-stream flowing between two hills from the place where we stood to the same broad, level glacier over which we had come in the ascent. The true source of the latter was, in fact, this ice-stream which flows down from the inland ice. We stood for a time at its edge, telescope in hand, discussing whether it would be

* Mount Chydenius is, however, north-*west* of Mount Edlund.

possible to descend by this apparently easy way, or whether we must go round by the longer route, somewhat dangerous as it was by reason of the hyperite cliff. A young "Balsfjording," who carried our instruments, and had certainly climbed many a mountain near his home, but probably never been on a glacier, looked at us with wondering eyes when we asked him his opinion. His expression seemed to say, "How can any one be in doubt about so obvious a matter?" Without a word, he sprang down the ice-slope, theodolite in hand, to our great terror, for we feared that, as usual, the glacier would be broken by crevasses, and difficult to cross. Our anxiety did not last long before we saw him come to a halt, and just in time, for, on coming nearer, we found that a great *schrund* was immediately before him. We crept to its edge and looked down into the weird, bottomless depth, whose walls were azure-blue cliffs of ice, here and there covered with white icicles like stalactites. Lower down everything was lost in a dark-blue gloom. This crevasse stretched almost the whole way across the glacier, so that a long detour had to be made before it could be crossed. Later on we encountered a great number of such crevasses, some of which we turned, others jumped over, others again crossed by ice-bridges. Not till we reached the main stream of the glacier did the crevasses come to an end and the descent became quick and easy."

On returning to the coast they took a boat and rowed to the mouth of Heley's Sound, some three miles north of which they landed in a little bay and set up their tent. Next day, August 22, was

ASCENT OF THE WHITE MOUNTAIN 45

again fine, so they set forth to make the ascent of the neighbouring White Mountain.

"We wandered first over the great moraine, which the glacier has cast down before itself, then climbed the gently sloping icefield. This proved to be unexpectedly fatiguing and disagreeable work. The surface consisted of thawed and refrozen snow, covered with a crust of faggot-like formation, which frequently broke up under our tread, so that the foot sank into the soft snow beneath and was with difficulty withdrawn through the icecrust, whose sharp edges cut into the boots. The top of the mountain, hidden at first by the humps of the glacier, came into view after an hour's ascent, but was still far away. We had several hours of work over snow of similar character before we reached the summit, a small plateau covered with powdery snow a foot deep upon hard ice.

"The view from this point is perhaps the finest to be found on Spitsbergen. In the east, about sixty miles away, we saw a high mountain land with two peaks higher than the rest. [This was Wiches Land.] Between it and Spitsbergen lay a sea covered with great, continuous icefloes, obviously impenetrable by a ship. . . . In the north-east and north, far as the eye could reach, appeared the hills of North-East Land and Hinloopen Strait, with the strait itself and its islands apparently surrounded by water free of ice. Nordenskiöld recognised Mount Lovén, ascended by him in 1861. . . . The interior was likewise displayed before our eyes, a boundless immeasurable waste of snow, out of which here and there some mass of rock jutted forth, dark in contrast with the blinding white surroundings. Only further away, west and north-west, were there any connected ranges of mountains. The whole west and north coasts of Wybe Jans Water were in sight, and the northern part of Barents Land, whose extreme point consists of a much crevassed snow-mountain ending steeply in the sea."

From this interesting digression we must return to our own doings. Facing south-east we kept along the crest of the highest ground and made quick progress, for a gentle slope drooped in our favour and the surface of the snow was in perfect condition for both ski and sledges. Garwood and I shall ever remember the delight of this midnight march. High above the clear air that surrounded us was a dark-blue roof of soft cloud, resting on skyey walls of marvellous colours, with streaks of stratus across them, reflecting the golden sunlight. The sun itself was hidden in the north, but beneath it hung a reticulated web, woven of gold and Tyrian purple, through which shafts of tender light drooped down like eyelashes upon the snow. All around, the *névé* went sweeping away in gentle curves and domes, greyish-white in some places with purple shadows, bluish-grey in others, here and there strewn with carpets of sunlight. The rocks, too, wherever they appeared, were rich in colour, showing their own ruddy or orange tints enforced by the lustrous atmosphere. There was none of the sharp contrast of black and white that strikes a superficial observer in high mountain views. This panorama was a glorious mass of colour, harmonious without rift and rich without monotony. Just at midnight the cloud-roof opened in the north and a flood of sunshine fell around and upon us—a veritable transfiguration and thrilling glory which cannot be told. Entranced with beauty, we marched on and on over the wide snowfield, with a sense of boundless space, a feeling of freedom, a joy as in the ownership of the whole universe—emotions that, in my experience, only arise in the great clean places of the earth, where nothing lives and nothing grows, the great deserts and the wide snowfields. Green country, after such regions, is land soiled by mildew.

Coming, in about seven miles march, to the point where the slope down to the Nordenskiöld Glacier began to steepen, we halted, not from fatigue, but because we were loath to quit the far-seeing uplands and wall ourselves in between a valley's sides. So we pitched the camp about 3 A.M., with the doors opening to the south. The eastward views were better displayed than before. We could see Wybe Jans Water with Barents Land beyond, then a series of long rock-faces supporting high-domed, snowy plateaus, stretching round to the Terrier on the left side of the

Nordenskiöld Glacier, whilst De Geer Peak came last, looking from this point like a pyramid with its top storey horizontally stratified. The low sun shone golden on the snowfield, casting blue shadows. All round, near the horizon, the sky was clear below the soft, thin cloud-roof, through which the blueness of the vault of heaven was plainly seen. The remote hills were indigo, patched with orange, gold, and pink. White mists lay in hollows of the snow, motionless. Ivory gulls flew about, projecting their silver plumage against the blue shadows. The air was still. Not a sound broke the perfection of the silence.

It was afternoon of the 19th when we set forward again over the good, hard snow, the still air seeming warm, and the sun shining softly behind a thin grey roof of cloud. All round was a light-blue frieze of sky with cloud-flakes in lines below, and then the faint blue-and-white hills. In the south the burnished surface of Klaas Billen Bay, shining between purple shores, reflected the sunlight. The beauty of the scene sapped our energies. We wanted to look at it, not to haul sledges. But Svensen said he could do no work, so hauling was the order of our day. Needless to say that many halts were made on every kind of excuse, and every halt was celebrated by the smoke of pipes. Garwood took the opportunity to instruct me in the true art of pipe-loading.

DESCENDING THE GLACIER 49

"Jam the tobacco in as tight as you can, and then loosen it with a corkscrew" is his formula. I am witness to the labour it cost him in practice, and the tenacity of his adherence to an adopted principle. One advantage of travelling with sledges is that you always have comfortable seats ready. It would have been a sin, at least a folly, not to avail ourselves of them. We were neither sinners nor fools after this kind. Yet on the whole good progress was made, for we walked fast and kept going for many hours. The view scarcely changed. That we were coming to lower levels was obvious, but the hills in front seemed no nearer after three hours' marching than at the start. Ahead were a few rocks emerging from the glacier. We thought them close at hand, but they kept their distance. Not for five hours were they left behind. The actual motion, however, was pleasant; ski and sledges often ran of themselves. Only Nielsen was miserable with his Canadian snowshoes, and perforce lagged behind. "This," he said, "is the worst thing ever a man put on his feet—miserables!" His own Lapp shoes, too, gave him no satisfaction. Melted snow found a way through them. "They should have been soaked," he said, "with two parts Stockholm tar and three parts cod-liver oil, boiled together and put on hot. It should be rubbed well in with a rag while it's hot. That will make boots waterproof and keep them soft for three months in spite of wettings. That is what our Norwegian fishermen use." Mr. Frederick Jackson, however, tells me that he tried this composition and found it no better than patent dubbin.

A flat plain followed a long and steady descent. Here, at a level of about 1300 feet, the snow began to be bad. A foot of new snow lay upon the ice. It was in places water-logged, for there were no open crevasses, and now the sun had attained power to set things thawing fast. The blue lakes we saw when coming up existed no more; drifted snow and frost had abolished them altogether. We were well below our camping place at the foot of Mount De Geer, but on the opposite side of the glacier, approaching its left bank. A wide water-channel came, with a rushing torrent in it, flowing over blue ice between banks of snow. It was long before we found an overhanging place where a leap would take a man from bank to bank. Thence a flat but watery area intervened before our goal was reached at the extreme left of the glacier and right below the highest point of the long Terrier ridge, to the summit of which we intended to climb next day. Its cliffs were loud with the sound of countless birds, whose full-throated cries, mingled together and wafted afar as a raucous hum, were audible long before a bird came in sight. From camp we could see them in their thousands, perched in rows upon ledges or soaring about the cliff—

CURIOUS ICE FORMATION

fulmars, little auks, and glaucus gulls. Their feathers were scattered all about, whilst numerous tracks showed that this breeding-place was no secret to the foxes—the only animals that rove over the icy interior of Spitsbergen.

Our projected climb was not to be made, for rain came on in the night. We awoke (20th) to find clouds heavy upon us, and all but the Terrier's foundations obliterated. It was a disappointment, but there were compensations, for the immediate neighbourhood proved unexpectedly interesting. This discovered, we loaded the sledges and sent them down with the men, under orders not to stop till they reached Klaas Billen Bay. Svensen had no longer any excuse for malingering. Yesterday, with every hour's advance, his face became rounder, his back straighter, his movements more active. The fear of destruction was in reality his main disease, aggravated no doubt by cold and exposure to the storm. He acknowledged as much later on. The suggestion that he should hasten down to the bay, whether dragging a sledge or not, seemed nothing less than a reprieve from sentence of death. He set off with alacrity.

Garwood had observed a curious piece of glacier a few hundred yards away from camp. It was mounded in a peculiar manner, calling for investigation. On approaching it, the mounds were perceived to be arches of ice, barrel vaults perfectly regular in form. Their origin was presently self-explained. A wide and deep stream of surface drainage-water habitually flows near the foot of the Terrier. Reaching a level place, the speed of flow is reduced so that the surface becomes frozen over in cold weather. Snow falls upon the ice thus formed, and a roof is made, the remains of which, even at this advanced period of the summer, were two feet thick or more. The glacier in its onward movement is compressed between the Terrier and the De Geer range opposite, and every portion of it feels this compression, which, operating on the frozen roof of the river, bends it up into an icy tunnel of regular form. By degrees parts of the tunnel fall in, and thus the detached arches are left. On the King's Bay Glacier we afterwards saw more arches of similar origin. It is to the strength of the arctic winter's frost, rather than to the amount of the annual snowfall, that Spitsbergen glaciers owe their peculiar phenomena, to which the glaciers of high mountain regions in the temperate and tropical parts of the world present no parallels.

Another and still more remarkable outcome of the same forces presently attracted our attention. We were descending the left side of the glacier below the Terrier and approaching the point at the end of the mountain where a great tributary glacier comes in from the east. The two ice-streams, joining, compress one another laterally, and cause a bulging or convexity of their surfaces, which only attain a common uniformity of level at a distance of a mile or so. By this means a triangular hollow is formed between the glaciers, and backed against the foot of the intervening hill. A lake collects in this hollow, and is drained by a stream, which, gradually cutting down its bed as the year advances, lowers the level of the lake. When the winter comes, fresh snow falls into and blocks this stream, damming back the waters so that the level of the lake rises. Its surface, of course, freezes; the ice-covering, with the thawed, refrozen collection of snow upon it, attaining a thickness of four feet and more. On the return of spring, when the snows begin to melt, fresh quantities of water find their way into the lake and raise the heavy ice-sheet. The bed of last year's streams is of course filled up with hard-frozen snow, so that there is no exit for the waters till the cup is full. The moment it begins to overflow the cutting of the channel takes place. The pent-up waters are let loose and evidently operate with extraordinary force, excavating a deep cañon out of the glacier. The floating ice acquires a momentum, whereby it not merely gets ripped and broken up, but forced forward on to the dry glacier ahead, great tables of it being turned up on end or piled on one another two or three deep. When most of the water is drawn off and the level of the lake is greatly reduced, the convulsion ceases and only the deep cañon and the wild ruin of the iceblocks, strewn abroad over half a mile square of the glacier, remain to show what mighty forces have been let loose.

During the summer we came upon several such burst lakes at the junctions of glaciers. The most striking of them was this one at the extremity of the Terrier, for, owing to the configuration of the ice, it is unusually large and, besides (like the Märjelen See by the Aletsch Glacier), is the receptacle into which many icebergs fall. These icebergs in the winter are frozen in, and tossed out in a wild ruin when the lake bursts. The chaos of strewn iceblocks is visible from far off, but its origin is not then discernible. Masses of ice were heaped against one another to a height of forty feet or even more. The blue cañon was so deep and undercut that we could not see to the bottom. It was more than sixty feet in depth. There was something inexpressibly weird in the silence and repose of this icy ruin surviving the wild turmoil of its birth. The catastrophe must have been recent, for the icebergs retained the blue colouring and transparency of their submerged parts. We spent a long time clambering about the *débris*, then hastened forward on our ski and caught up with the sledges.

A lunch halt was made at the top of a steeper slope, just where crevasses began to be numerous. By keeping well round to the left their intricacy was easily avoided. Where the descent was made they were relatively small and for the most part wedged with winter snow, strong enough to bear. Leaving the men to guide the sledges down, we gaily shot the slope, crevasses and all, on our ski. Though the ice was rough and much honeycombed, we covered a mile of descent in a few minutes, "everything safely," as our dragoman used to say on the Nile in a gale of wind. At the foot, where the glacier became more level, prosaic marching order had to be resumed. Klaas Billen Bay was nearing, a leaden purple, almost black expanse, dotted over with countless icebergs in the gloomy beclouded evening light. The final descent over the steep moraine was even more difficult than the ascent, for the useful snow-strip had melted away and the stones were more unstable than before. The sledges were seriously knocked about in the process of lowering; the metal covering of the runners was stripped off and the runners themselves smashed in two places. They just held together so that we could drag them over the *débris* fan and the wide bog beyond to where our camp was standing uninjured, with the whaleboat drawn up beside it.

The general result of this inland excursion was highly satisfactory, notwithstanding our misfortune with Svensen. It enabled us to record in outline the general structure of the area included between Wijde Bay, Dickson Bay, Ice Fjord, Wybe Jans Water, and Hinloopen Strait. Before the recently undertaken exploration of the interior, Spitsbergen was supposed to be covered, like Greenland, with a big icesheet. There were known to be some mountains, but they were described as nunataks—islands of rock poked up through the enveloping ice. The nature of the Greenland icesheet is well known; it buries the whole interior beneath its vast thickness, hiding hills and valleys together within its mass, and flowing down over them on all sides to the sea, toward or into which it sends tongues of ice through every gap. All the glaciers in Greenland are but tongues of a single icesheet. Spitsbergen was supposed to resemble Greenland in this respect. In 1896 we proved this view to be erroneous as to the central portion of the island. The belt of land bounded on the south by Bell Sound and on the north by Ice Fjord, and stretching across from sea to sea, is absolutely devoid of any icesheet. It is a complex of mountains and valleys, amongst which are many glaciers indeed, as there are amidst the mountains of Central Europe, but no continuous covering of ice. Each glacier is a separate unit, having its own catchment area and drainage system. The valleys are boggy and relatively fertile, the hillsides bare of snow in summer up to more than 1000 feet above sea-level.

THE COLORADO PLATEAU.

NO TRUE ICESHEET

There are lines of depression between Ice Fjord and Bell Sound, and between Sassen Bay and the east coast, which are absolutely snow-free throughout the arctic summer.

We had a suspicion that the area between Foreland Sound and Ice Fjord was not covered by an icesheet, but we still thought it probable that one would be found in the region north-east of Ice Fjord. The result of our present expedition was to prove this not to be the case. We traversed a great deal of glacier and snowfield, but none belonging to a true icesheet. The whole of this region, which I have named Garwood Land, after my excellent companion, is a glaciated mountain and valley system. Each glacier in it is a clearly-marked unit, with its evident watersheds dividing it from its neighbours. North of the Chydenius range, by which Garwood Land is bounded, there does come a true icesheet covering the whole of New Friesland and flowing down to the sea on all sides. North-East Land, too, is buried under an icesheet. These are the only ones in the Spitsbergen archipelago.

The mountains of Garwood Land are remains of a denuded plateau, resembling those of the Sassendal region. They have been carved out by a denuding agent eating a series of valleys back into the plateau. Readers of my former book, "The First Crossing of Spitsbergen," will remember how many examples of the rapid formation and extension of valleys by the eating back of the head-waters are there recorded. The Colorado Berg north of the Sassendal was the best example of the process. That plateau, now bare of ice, is being rapidly cut up into separate hills by the excavation of a series of deep, narrow cañons, which will widen and creep further back year by year. Now, the hills of Garwood Land are of a similar type. The wide, deep valley, into the head of which we looked down from our farthest point, sends back into the plateau (or remnant of a plateau) a number of tributary valleys, all of the same deep, gently sloping, steep-headed type. From many indications we concluded that a series of similar valley-heads and cliffs lay to the eastward of our whole route from where we turned back as far as the Terrier. This row of cliffs and bluffs probably flanks the eastern watershed of the Nordenskiöld Glacier. The bad weather that prevented our ascent of the Terrier prevented also the verification of this hypothesis.

If we could assume that Garwood Land was at any time considerably less glacier-covered than it now is, so that its valleys were bog-bottomed like the Sassendal, and its uplands resembled the Colorado Berg, it would be easy to account for the present configuration of the land surface. We should say that it was formed by aqueous denudation, and subsequently covered up by the increase of the ice. It is certain that there has

LAND MODELLING

been a great increase in the ice-supply on the land hereabouts during the last two centuries, for in that time the Negri Glacier has advanced at least fifteen, probably twenty, miles into the sea along a front fifteen miles in width. This fact, however, does not suffice as foundation for so great an assumption. It is rather to the steady elevation of the land that we must look for a solution. Everywhere in Franz Josef Land and Spitsbergen the land is known to be rising. The western belt of the island has been longer exposed to denudation than the east belt. The latter, therefore, has perhaps been later elevated. It came up from the sea as relatively flat ground. As its elevation continued this flat ground was raised into a plateau. At first it did not reach the level of perpetual snow, so that whilst rising it was being cut down into valleys and cañons by the action of water, pouring off from the plateau over its edge, and hurrying down a frost-split rock-face. The bed of such a valley has of necessity a very gentle slope. The head is steep, almost a cliff, the whole face of which is being continually stripped off, so that the valley, once begun by a waterfall over the edge of the horizontally stratified plateau, penetrates steadily backward.

These valleys once formed, with their steep heads and sides, would maintain themselves even after the remains of the plateau were covered with an icesheet and the valleys filled with glaciers. There is no need to predicate for the glaciers any power of erosion; that is not the way arctic icesheets act, for the upper layers of ice flow over the lower at a far greater speed than is the case in glaciers under lower latitudes. Given an existing cliff, however, with a glacier below it, and the denuding agencies of frost and water at work upon it, that cliff tends to maintain itself and to eat its way back into the mountain mass behind, for its *débris* fall upon the glacier below and are carried away; they do not pile themselves up into a protecting slope at the base of the cliff. This eating-back process will go forward with unequal speed according to the varying qualities of the rocks. Bays will thus be formed and will eat back into the plateau, just as the gullies eat back in the Sassendal region, only the bays will tend to grow wider in proportion to their depth in a glaciated country than in a region mainly bare of snow and ice.

For this process to begin it is necessary that somewhere a rock-face should be exposed to the air. The exposure may be produced by a fault, or by a denuding process begun before the land was much glaciated. We are in no position yet to assert how the process commenced in Garwood Land, but that the bays, valleys, and cliffs now existing are being maintained in the manner above described is certain. If the ice were again

CONTRAST WITH GREENLAND

to cover up the Colorado Berg and the hills opposite, and were to flow into and down the Sassendal to Sassen Bay, the aspect of that region would resemble that of Garwood Land to-day. It is only in the case of a country like Greenland, entirely buried under an icecap thousands of feet thick, through which, save along the coast, no rock appears and no cliff is exposed—it is only in such a country that the conservative action of ice is complete and the modelling of an elevated land-mass into hills is practically arrested. Hence the scientific importance of distinguishing between a proper icesheet (in the Greenland sense) and a mere assemblage of separate glaciers, however large in volume and intimate in their connexion with one another. An icesheet, or inland-ice, operates in a totally different manner from a series of glaciers. Save in North-East Land and in the part of Spitsbergen called New Friesland, there is no proper icesheet in Spitsbergen, and the phrase "inland-ice" should be expunged from maps and descriptions of regions to which it is not applicable. A chief and no unimportant result of our explorations in the interior of Spitsbergen is this discovery that the parts supposed to be enveloped in an icesheet are in fact merely glacier regions.

CHAPTER IV

BY WATER TO KINGS BAY

On awaking in relative luxury, by the shore of Klaas Billen Bay, late in the afternoon of July 21, we were far from pushing eagerly forward to the labours of the day. It seemed so good to be in a well-stored camp, with no need to husband fuel or count teaspoonfuls of cocoa and sugar or fills of tobacco. Moreover, our wet clothes were drying over a lamp in the men's tent, drying all too thoroughly indeed, for Svensen permitted the soles to be burnt off the stockings. A final visit was made to the glacier-foot to photograph the wonderful cliff. Every prominent feature noticed a week before had fallen away, including a huge cavern that penetrated far into the solid mass of the ice. Returning to camp, Garwood found trilobites in a section of rock by the shore, and they were good excuse for further lingering. Ultimately the boat was hauled into the water, camp struck, and baggage loaded. The men rowed round the spit while we walked across to De Geer's camping-ground. At 10.30 P.M. they took us on board and we made sail for Advent Bay.

It was a feeble attempt at sailing, for no sooner did we really quit the shore than the last puff of wind died away. A beautiful mist hung low near the calm water, which presently became utterly smooth like a mirror of polished steel. There was just a purple line of shore on either hand dividing the roof of cloud from its reflection. De Geer's signals, built on his trigonometrical points along the level coast, alone broke its uniformity. Far, far away the peaks of the Dead Man appeared in blue and sunshine on the horizon. Without rowing no progress was to be made. At 3 A.M. we were opposite the mouth of Skans Bay. Countless birds were resting all around on the still water—puffins in pairs, like lovers always near to one another ; little auks, the babies of the feathery tribe ; fulmar petrels, the strong youths ; terns, the fair maidens ; skuas, the inquisitive old maids ; guillemots, the populace ; glaucous gulls, the police. A flock of fulmars kept us company, flying about and across, then settling on the water ahead to await our slow advance. When we caught up with them, flap and run, off they went again. This game pleased their minds and wings for an hour or more.

Spitsbergen weather makes for itself an undeservedly bad reputation. For example, the low roof of cloud that hung above us all this night, however beautiful the colouring cast by it on the landscape, and it was gorgeous beyond words, certainly produced an effect of gloom. It was long before we discovered how thin was the layer of mist, thin as well as low lying, and that above it all the hills were shining in brilliant sunlight. Through occasional small holes a peak or crest would appear, so incredibly bright as to seem actually aglow with internal fire. Behind us the fog lay upon the water, but ahead the hills across Ice Fjord were clear, and sunshine lured us on. Camp was to be pitched on one of the Goose Islands—that we had long decided; the only trouble was that the islands would not approach. We rowed and rowed, but they were coy. One might have sworn that they were drifting away. All of a sudden they changed their minds and neared us so rapidly that, when next we turned round, they were close at hand. They consist of diabase, with surface cut low and polished by ice into gentle undulations. Bog has collected in the hollows and there are a few pools. The sea front all round is a low cliff of dark, shattered rocks. Entering a narrow sound between the two larger islands, we came into an admirable land-locked harbour with an old camping-place close by. Garwood went after eider-ducks for dinner, whilst I saw to the domestic arrangements. The soft ground proved to be a quagmire, so we had to camp in the wet, choosing a spot close by a well-built fireplace, over which big whalebones had been crossed to carry the pot. The last visitors, a year ago, had kindly left for us a good pile of cut-up firewood ready at hand. No sooner was the fire burning well than a smart breeze sprang up, now that it could not serve for sailing, and blew straight into the fireplace, carrying the smoke directly over to the tents. The same breeze cleared away the clouds and brought sunshine indeed, but was the father of many out-compensating discomforts.

After a long sleep, breakfast was eaten at 6 P.M. (July 22) in a grey-toned, blustery evening. An hour was devoted to wandering over the islands. They are the home of many birds, especially eiders, which breed there in multitudes, making their nests upon the ground. We filled a large bag with down. Many of the nests were just abandoned and there were lots of young birds about—terns, geese, and skuas come on a visit, as well as the common enemy and scavenger, the glaucous, whom the ducks saluted with angry quacking. On shelves of a little diabase cliff I found a bevy of snow-buntings, most charming of arctic dicky-birds. Brilliant yellow lichens made the rocks gaudy with flaming colour. The bogs were the greenest I ever saw, whilst in drier places the flower carpet was as bright as Alice's in Wonderland. On a clear, calm day this would be a lovely spot for dawdling, the islands being grandly placed for views straight up Klaas Billen and Sassen bays and down Ice Fjord. But the chilly evening was not favourable for contemplation. I only remember noticing with pleasure the fine, gable-fronted crest of some precipitous limestone peaks which look down on Klaas Billen Bay and prolong into it the characteristic structure of Temple Mountain and its neighbours.

We sailed away about 7.30 P.M., with a moderate breeze coming out of Sassen Bay. How so little wind could put such a topple on to the sea I could not understand, but so it always is in the inner parts of Ice Fjord. Sitting still in the boat, we were soon miserably chilled down. Conversation flagged. Svensen expressed the general gloom by singing a slow and solemn Norwegian hymn in a deep bass voice. It seemed to cheer him, for he followed it up with a more mundane melody, sung in an uncertain falsetto. Thereupon the Cambridge contingent gave tongue with " The River Cam," which drifted into a topical song, endlessly prolonged, whereof the chorus lingers in my memory yet:

> Sailing away over Sassen Bay,
>   Where the waters are always rough,
> If pleasure you take as you shiver and shake,
>   You'll jolly soon have enough.

In three hours Ice Fjord was crossed and the beginning of the line of cliffs approached, west of

Hyperite Hat. Here the wind failed, just where it always used to fail last year. A long row transferred the heavy boat to the low point outside the mouth of Advent Bay, down which a stiff breeze was hurrying. We sailed across to the farther shore, where I landed to walk to the tourist-hut, leaving Garwood, who is an enthusiastic sailor—which I am not—to beat round Advent Point to the landing-place.

The inn contained a merry party, just returned in the *Kvik* from a visit to Lomme Bay, Wahlenburg's Bay, and Wijde Bay. They were full of pleasant talk and recent reminiscences of walrus, seal, and reindeer hunting. With their help our camp was soon pitched and our goods landed. More than three hours could not be spared to slumber, for, at 7.30 A.M. on the 23rd, the tourist steamer *Lofoten* came in from Norway, bringing mails. With her came perfect sunshine and delightful warmth. Not, indeed, that there was any time for mere pleasure. I had a solar observation to take, the baggage to overhaul, and a mail to despatch, whilst all was to be prepared for sailing next day in the *Kvik* for Kings Bay. There was no hitch.

In due course Advent Bay was again left behind, and we were on our way down Ice Fjord, once more with a few companions. Among them were the Swedish botanist, Herr Ekstam, and Mr. Baldwin, who was in Greenland with Lieut. Peary. Ekstam was to be left at Coles Bay, which I was thus enabled to visit. It is a dreary place, with a great extent of bogflat at its head, stretching far inland up a wide, desolate valley. At the end appears to be a pass to Low Sound. There are several similar valleys extending westward, one more uninviting than another. I suppose the bog near the bay is "Coles Park, a good place for venison, well known to Thomas Ayers," as Pelham says, writing in 1631. Coal having in recent years been found in the bay, the name has been confused from Coles to Coal.

In the smallest hours of the morning of the 25th the *Kvik* entered Foreland Sound. I have traversed this waterway from end to end on four separate occasions without experiencing clear weather. This time there was the usual cloud-roof, but it was high, so that we became in some degree acquainted with the remarkably fine scenery of the passage. The mountain tops were covered, but the glaciers were disclosed, and it is the glaciers that give to the sound its distinctive character. At first they are only on the east coast, a series draining the mountains north of the Dead Man. When these come to an end there follows a dull front of bare slopes as far as the opening of St. John's Bay, the Osborne's Inlet of the early charts. The southern quarter of the Foreland, if the Saddle Mountain at its south cape be excepted, consists of a plain, almost absolutely flat, and raised but a few feet above sea-level. It may be called Flatland. I have been told that Russian trappers used to frequent it; but there does not appear to be any published account whatever of a landing on it. No more featureless or uniform expanse can be conceived. It covers an area of fifty square miles, according to the chart, which, however, is most inaccurate hereabouts. This plain is indicated by nature as *the* place for laying out a base whenever Spitsbergen shall be used for the measurement of a meridian arc. North of Flatland comes a well-defined mountain group containing fine peaks. It is bounded by a deep depression running from Peter Winter's Bay in a south-west direction, right across the Foreland to the ocean. Peter Winter's Bay is well to the north of St. John's Bay, though marked south of it on the chart. It is indicated correctly enough by Giles and Reps on the remarkable Dutch chart published after 1707 by Gerard van Keulen. There it is named Zeehonde Bay, whilst a secluded anchorage in its north coast, just within the entrance, bears the designation Pieter Winter's Baaytje. North of Peter Winter's and St. John's bays the glaciers follow one another in quick succession on both shores. On the east there are eight of them between St. John's and English bays, whereof the two biggest, at the north and south ends, reach the sea. The opposite coast of the Foreland is an almost continuous glacier-front backed by a wall of snowy peaks.* The shallow place which stopped Barents and renders the channel impassable, except by small vessels, is off this glacier-front. The *Expres* used to run over it and bump if she felt inclined. The *Kvik* was navigated more gingerly, so that the passage over the Bar occupied a couple of hours, soundings being diligently taken all the time.

At the head of English Bay is a great glacier, flowing from the south-east and receiving many tributaries, noted later on. North of it come prominent hills with a wide lowland stretched before them, ending in a flat point named Quade Hook—that is, "the Evil Cape." Rounding this cape, we slipped into Kings Bay and steered for its head, across the whole breadth of which was the great front of the Kings Glacier awaiting its first explorers. Clouds hung low down, and there was no distant view inland, not so much indeed as we had seen the previous year. We afterward came to know it well, so for clearness' sake I may take the liberty of brushing the clouds away and describing the general arrangement of the hills and glaciers, with which the reader is invited to make closer acquaintance in the following pages.

* These are continued northward by some lower snowy hills ending in the bold Fair Foreland or Birds' Cape.

Let him, then, return with me to the mouth of the bay, and, standing there, face to the east, with Quade Hook on his right hand. He will be looking straight up the bay. On his left hand will be Mitra Hook, so named from the pointed mitre peak which Scoresby climbed. This exit to the sea between Mitra and Quade hooks is common to both Kings and Cross bays, which are divided from one another by a rectangular mountain mass. Cross Bay is unknown to me. It is said to be one of the finest bays in Spitsbergen. The mountains on either side of it are steep, and magnificent glaciers fall into its head, one of them ending in the finest icecliff in this part of the world. Cross Bay runs in to the north, Kings Bay to the east. Kings Bay is broad at first, with low, flat coasts, beyond which mountains rise to a moderate height. Farther in, the sides approach somewhat, where there is a low cape to the south with Coal Haven and some islands just round the corner, whilst on the north is the protruding hilly mass of Blomstrand's Mound, five or six hundred feet high, with a cove at each end of it (Blomstrand's Harbour to the west, Deer Bay to the east), and in each cove a glacier ending in the sea. It is not till this narrower place has been traversed that the splendour of Kings Bay is fully beheld. Within, the bay is a circle about six miles in diameter, ringed around with an almost continuous series of glaciers, whereof only those on the south are cut off from the sea by a belt of low-lying ground. Scattered about the inner bay are Lovén's Islands, some of which we shall presently visit. On the south the mountains are of bold and pointed form. They are the watershed between Kings and English bays. On the north, however, is a far more noble group, culminating in two peaks that resemble the Dom and Täschhorn of Zermatt. These peaks are small, of course, but they look no whit less fine than their Alpine fellows, and no one acquainted with the Alps would guess them to be smaller than peaks of the great range. From and about these mountains flow magnificent glaciers, whose upper ramifications were too complicated to be sketched on the map from so distant an inspection. The remainder of the view, the whole eastward end of the bay, is occupied by the face of a single mighty glacier, splendid beyond exaggeration. It is no smooth expanse of ice, but a splintered and broken torrent, which submerges islands of rock and flows over or about them with tortuous and tormented sweep. A few miles in, this glacier divides, just as Cross and Kings bays divide, the wider constituent being the Crowns Glacier, coming from the north, the other the King's Highway, up which you go to the south-east. Between them is the mountain mass, whereof the famous Three Crowns are the

LANDING IN KINGS BAY

most remarkable, though not the highest peaks. Of course there are plenty of minor tributary glaciers, as the reader will learn soon enough; one only need be mentioned. It runs into the midst of the Crowns group and divides it in half, separating the Three Crowns on the north from the Pretender and the Two Queens on the south. Up this glacier lies the shortest route across the land from Kings to Ekman bay. If the reader has comprehended so dull a geographical description, he can understand our general line of route in exploring this most beautiful and interesting region, which seems to be intended by Nature for the arctic " Playground of Europe."

Advancing up the bay in the *Kvik*, we could see little of the wonderful panorama. Clouds hid the Crowns and all but the bases of the nearer hills. As our intention was to make our way inland, we required to be put ashore at the best point for climbing on to the glacier. We headed, therefore, for the middle of the face, where an island of rock rises partly out of the sea, partly through the ice. It soon became apparent that this would not do, for the glacier all round it was broken into such a chaos of seracs as to be absolutely untraversable in any direction. One could only land at the north or south angle of the bay. The north angle might have suited, but the slopes behind it seemed steep to drag sledges up; we therefore chose the south. I am not sure that we chose right. The inner part of the bay was dotted over with floating masses of ice fallen from the glacier. They became more numerous the farther we advanced. At last the skipper said he could not venture on, so our boat was lowered and the baggage stowed into it. After bidding adieu to our friends and arranging with the captain to call for us at midnight, August 11-12, we rowed away.

It was high tide, so there were no falls taking place from the long glacier-front, which was fortunate, seeing that we had to pass pretty close under it. The cliff was even finer than that of the Nordenskiöld Glacier, because it was more splintered. At 5 P.M. we came ashore on the end of a fan of stone and mud *débris*, laid down by a stream just in front of the left foot of Kings Glacier. The glacier ends on this fan with a curving moraine-covered slope, by which access could be attained to a relatively smooth surface leading inwards in the direction we desired to take. The boat was hauled up, the baggage dragged and carried about a hundred yards inland to the nearest suitable camping-ground. Necessary arrangements occupied the remainder of the day. The sun bursting through the cloud-roof illuminated the glacier-front with fine splashes of light, manifesting its blue caverns and silver spires. Thundering falls of ice presently set in and followed one another in rapid succession, now near at hand, now far away. A big iceberg was stranded on the shore just off our point, and a number of fulmars settled down upon it and went to sleep. Amidst such surroundings there was always plenty of entertainment, besides that delightful expectation of the unknown and unforeseen which is said to have bedevilled Ulysses.

CHAPTER V

THE KING'S HIGHWAY

THE next morning (July 26), being beautifully fine, was devoted to an astronomical determination of our position and other preparations for carrying on a survey. A preliminary expedition up the glacier occupied the afternoon. An easy way was found on to the ice, but there luck turned, for, as a matter of fact, we were not really on the Kings Glacier itself, but on the foot of a small tributary flowing round from an enclosed basin on the south and divided from the main glacier by an immense moraine. This moraine would have to be crossed; we knew enough of dragging sledges over moraines to foresee something of the troubles thus provided. We wandered over the small glacier to the foot of a peak standing in the angle between it and the Highway. Then Garwood and Nielsen set off to climb the peak (Mount Nielsen 3120 ft.) by its rotten *arête*, whilst I with Svensen went on to investigate the moraine and find the best way over it. Returning the first to camp, I sat in the door, watching the wonder of the glacier's terminal cliff, its bold towers, tottering pinnacles, and sections of crevasses with fallen blocks wedged into their jaws. Lumps of ice were continually falling. Fortunate enough to be gazing in the right direction, I saw a monster pinnacle come down. First a few fragments were crushed out from right and left near its base; then the whole tower seemed to sink vertically, smashing up within as it gave way, and finally toppling over and shooting forward into the water, which it dashed aloft. The resulting wave spread and broke around, hurling the floating blocks against one another, and upsetting the balance of many. Its widening undulation could be traced far away by the stately courtesy of the rocking icebergs. The front of the cliff was barred across with sunlight and shadow, throwing into relief this and the other icy pinnacle, above some blue wall or gloomy cavern. Behind the wall the glacier was not smooth, but broken into a tumult of seracs, like the most ruinous icefall in the Alps, as far as the eye could reach. Varying illumination on this splintered area evoked all manner of resemblances for the play of a vagrant imagination. Sometimes the glacier looked like an innumerable multitude of white-robed penitents, sometimes like the tented field of a great army, sometimes like a frozen cataract. Its suggestiveness was boundless, its beauty always perfect; moreover, it was worthily framed. The mountains that enclose it are fine in form, with splintered ridges, steep *couloirs*, and countless high-placed glaciers, caught on ledges or sweeping down to join the great ice-river.

Garwood returned full of a satisfaction which Nielsen heartily shared. The scramble had been exhilarating, the view superb. There was no ice-sheet visible, only mountains everywhere, with glaciers between. The moraine once passed, our way was open ahead up ice apparently smooth. After supper I set out alone in the opposite direction along the shore, for the purpose of starting the plane-table survey from a well-marked eminence near the foot of the second side-glacier, whose black, terminal slope curves round and up with singular regularity of form. The walk was beautiful, the ice-dappled sea being always close at hand with noble hills beyond. There were plenty of torrents to wade, besides one which had to be jumped. It flows down a gully cut sharply into the dolomite rock. Below the glacier are ice-worn rocks, both rounded and grooved; but the direction of the grooves is at right-angles to that of the axis of the glacier, so that they appear to have been scratched when the main Kings Glacier extended thus much farther and higher. Returning, I kept close along the margin of the bay. Innumerable fragments of crystal-clear ice, each filled with sunshine, danced in the breaking ripples. The water splashed amongst them, singing a cheerful song which was altogether new to me. The cliff-front of the glacier ahead was darkened with shadow, and represented a battlemented wall with deep portals leading through to a white marble city within.

On the following day, sun brightly shining and breezes blowing fresh, we loaded up two sledges with food for ten days, and set forth up the King's Highway. A laborious struggle took the sledges past the terminal moraine, but the ice beyond was dotted with frequent stones, so that the runners were generally foul of one or more. The slope was very steep. Reaching a more level place, we encountered ice so humpy that the sledges were always on their noses or their tails. Then came a cañon, 50 feet or so deep, and about 20 feet wide. We had to track alongside of it in an undesired direction till a doubtful-looking bridge was found, over which a passage could be risked. More lumpy ice followed till we were level with the foot of Mount Nielsen, where a smoother area was entered on. Here I left the caravan and climbed to the top of a hump on the *arête* of the peak to continue the survey. My solitary industry was enlivened by the neighbourhood of countless nesting birds, snow buntings, little auks, and guillemots, whose home is in the cliffs. Thus far the big moraine was close by on our left hand, mountains on our right; the level stretch of ice led between the two to the meeting of moraine and mountain at the entrance of the next side valley beyond Mount Nielsen. Here the stone-strip had to be crossed. I came up with the others just as the crossing began. We thought the moraine belt at this point would be but a few yards in width. It was more than half a mile. We only found that out after unloading the sledges and taking every man his burden. They were carried over, a return made for more, the process repeated, and so on for two whole hours—a heartbreaking experience. It was a hilly moraine or set of moraines, with two main ascents and descents besides several minor undulations. Footing was, of course, on loose stones only. In such places laden men slip about, bark their shins, twist their ankles, and lose their tempers. Beyond the stones came humpy ice again, ridged into short, steep undulations. A sledge required vigorous hoisting over each of them, the distance from trough to trough being about five yards, and the ridges transverse to our line of route. "On every hump," said Nielsen, "a sledge capsizes." Certainly one sledge or the other was generally rolling over on its back. After six hours of hard work we agreed to camp (460 feet)—"the hardest day's work I've done in a long time," was Nielsen's comment, and we believed him, for he put his back into it with hearty goodwill. Only when the tents were pitched had we leisure to enjoy the

AN EASY PLACE

warm sunshine and the exhilarating, absolutely calm air. Out on the ice we could sit in our shirt-sleeves without being chilled. All around spread the great glacier in its beauty; the sky overhead was blue; the bay reflected the sunshine; fleeces of mist adorned the hilltops. In that perfect hour we craved for nothing save the company of absent friends.

The next day (July 28) we made good progress, ascending 720 feet and covering a long distance. None of it was easy-going; in fact, when you have sledges to drag there is no easy going except on the flat. Every stage of a glacier has its own troubles. First comes the steep snout and its moraine, then humpy ice and open crevasses, next honeycomb ice and water-holes, which gradually pass (in fine melting weather) into glacier covered by waterlogged snow. We began the day with honeycomb ice and water-holes. The honeycomb ice on the Nordenskiöld Glacier made rather good travelling; it was otherwise on the King's Highway. Several fine days had flooded the surface with water, so that, where crevasses ceased and the water had no downward outlet, it was obliged to trickle about, forming pools, rills, and rivers, all in different ways perplexing to the traveller. The cells of the honeycomb ice were thus full of water, and, as they gave way under the pressure of a tread, the foot crunched through into water at every step. By slow degrees the honeycomb was replaced by sodden snow, which grew steadily deeper as we advanced to higher levels. Here the whole surface shone in the sunlight, for the water oozed about in pools and sluggish streams, forming square miles of slush. There were brief intervals of dryness where the surface rose in some perceptible slope, but they were short, the almost flat waterlogged areas covered the larger part of the region to be traversed. If the march was uncomfortable and toilsome, each could laugh at the antics of the others. We steered a devious route, seeking to follow the white patches and to avoid the glassy blue areas where water actually came to the surface. But all that looked white was not solid. You would see the leader shuffling gingerly forward on his ski, trying to pretend that he was a mere bubble of lightness. Suddenly, through he would go up to the knee, the points of his ski would catch in the depths and a mighty floundering ensue. The sledges got into similar fixes, and often added to the confusion by rolling over most inopportunely. The leading sledge usually served to indicate a way to be avoided, so, before very long, the two parties wandered asunder and enjoyed one another's struggles and perplexities from a distance.

It is obvious that Nature must provide some sort of a drainage system for such a quantity of water. The bogs and pools leak into one another and by degrees cut channels with ill-defined banks of snow, along which the current slowly crawls. By union of such streams strong-flowing torrents are formed; these make deep cuttings into the glacier and unite into a trunk river, deep, swift, and many yards wide. Every uncrevassed side glacier above the snowline pours out a similar river on to the surface of the main glacier, and these rivers in their turns presently join the trunk stream. Thus, whatever route you take, whether you keep near the trunk stream or far from it, the side streams have to be crossed. The crossing of them is often a tough business. Their icebanks are about twelve feet high and usually vertical; their volume of water is too considerable to be waded, seeing that their beds are of smooth, slippery, blue ice, on which footing cannot be maintained for a moment. They are seldom less than four yards wide. The blue strip with the clear water between the white walls is always a lovely sight, but to a traveller quite as tantalising. A crossing can only be accomplished where the water has chanced to undercut one of the banks and at the same time to leave a level place beside it at the foot of the other bank. You can then jump over with some hope of gaining a footing where you land. The sledges have to follow with a perilous bump. Rarely you may find a snowbridge. In search of possible crossings we had to travel alongside of these streams, time and again, far out of our line of route, whilst, to make matters worse, it happened that we were on the wrong side of the trunk river; thus that also had to be crossed, a problem apparently insoluble, till a great and well-blessed bridge was found just at the end of the day's march.

Nielsen worked like a horse all day long, his full weight thrown forward and his body inclined at a surprising angle. Svensen, by the gestures of his arms and the sorry expression of his countenance, looked as if he were labouring exceedingly, but of his towering frame the vertical was the customary attitude, and if the one of us who was sharing his sledge left off pulling for a moment the sledge mysteriously stuck fast. There were, indeed, signs of a return of Svensen's malady; but it was explained to him that, regard being had to the comfortable warmth of the weather and absence of wind, his health was not to be deranged, and that, if it should happen that he could not go on with us, doing his full share of work, he would have to find his way back to the coast alone. Thenceforward he throve exceedingly, and only penalised us by "sugaring" when not closely watched.

The character of the scenery changed considerably during the progress of the march. Our first camp looked up both the Crowns and Highway glaciers and was opposite the big nunatak which divides them. It is a true nunatak, or hilltop rising from the bed of the glacier, not an entire mountain surrounded by different glaciers. At one time it must have been buried under ice, for all its top seems to be moutonnised. The Crowns and Queens groups were both well seen from the same camp, or would have been but for a few clouds. As we advanced, the Crowns disappeared behind the Pretender and Queens, and we came under the rounded and bare south slopes of these—a dull prospect. But new objects of interest were appearing in the other direction, where the Highway Glacier widened out and branched off into white bays and tributaries, separated from one another by peaks of striking and precipitous form, finely grouped. When the Three Crowns were finally hidden, there opened out on the left side of the Highway a broad valley, south-westward, that bent round to the west and soon reached a wide snow pass, beyond which, still curving round, it led down to the glacier emptying into the head of English Bay.

All day long we were rounding away from the purple fjord and visibly leaving it behind, though the distance to the watershed in front did not perceptibly diminish. The weather continued fine, though not clear; the sun peeped through the mottled sky from time to time, but fogs rolled about like big snowballs on the higher *névés*. Camp was pitched (1180 feet) in the midst of the widest part of the glacier about a mile below the point where it bifurcates, each branch leading up to a wide snow pass of its own. The north branch continues the direction of the lower part of the glacier, so we decided to go to it. A widening wedge of peaks divides the cols, and coming down to a sharp *arête* buries itself beneath the ice at Junction Point (named because it must be referred to again in the course of this narrative).

The 29th was a glorious day. Resolutions were made that we would march on to the watershed, whatever its distance. It is as easy to change these resolves in the afternoon as to make them in the morning. The pools of water were now left behind, but the snow on the surface of the ice was still sodden and slushy. In the first three-quarters of an hour we rose 120 feet, and reached the end of the ridge at Junction Point. Rocks were here disclosed, so Garwood went off geologising. The rest of us plunged into an island of fog, and hauled on up a steep slope, where the snow became good, and thenceforward remained in perfect condition for ski at that and all higher levels. Without ski it would have been impossible to do much, for we should have sunk up to, or above, the knee in snow, over which, with them, we slid in luxury. Above this slope the fog ended, and a wide, very gently sloping plain of snow followed, stretching afar on all sides. This is the highest basin and gathering ground of the glacier. It is almost level with the passes that divide the mountains on the north. If we had but known that the same is true of the *névé* on the other side of those passes, we might have saved ourselves the long round of a few days later. Now that there was no water to trouble us, we suffered acutely from thirst, for the day was quite hot and the sun burned fiercely. We peeled off our garments one by one and rejoiced in an unwonted freedom.

The mountains bordering the King's Highway average somewhat over 3000 feet in height. As the level of the glacier rises, the lower slopes are more deeply covered and the visible remainder of the peaks comes to be not much above 1000 feet. They appear, moreover, to stand wider apart from one another, and the glacier, filling the valley more deeply, becomes itself considerably wider. Nevertheless, such is the fine form of the mountains that they still appear large, especially to an eye trained in greater ranges. Being themselves magnified, they proportionally magnify the aspect of the glacial expanse, which pretends to be of quite enormous extent—a spotless desert of purest white. The views on all sides were of entrancing beauty, especially the view back down the blue vista of Kings Bay. The broad white col ahead seemed for hours little elevated above us. There were far, coy, tantalising peaks over and beyond. From the col itself rose a small mound, perhaps 500 feet high, by the foot of which it was our intention to camp, but hour passed after hour, and it never seemed nearer.

Busied with the survey, perforce I lagged behind and was alone in the midst of a world of whiteness. A lengthening shadow was my sole moving companion, save when some stray fulmar petrel came whizzing by, *en route* from Kings Bay to Ice Fjord. The tracks of foxes were crossed not infrequently, but no fox did I actually see. At 9 P.M. the col was apparently as far off as ever, and Nielsen had done as much work as a man could be expected to do in a day. Svensen didn't count, as he always put on the aspect of a moribund person. He expressed a full agreement with Nielsen's ejaculation, "We'll have to have plenty of soup for this." Ultimately we gave up till the morrow the resolved pursuit of the pass and camped at a height of 2170 feet, having risen about 1000 feet during the day. The first thing done was to melt snow for a debauch. Deep were our potions; the insipid draught tasted for once like divine nectar. The sun continued his bright shining and the tents were warm within. We lay on our bags, enjoying the simple beauty of the view seen through the open door. Each deep-trodden footprint in front was a cup filled with a shadow of purest blue, pale like the sky. A white expanse followed, slightly mottled with blue in the foreground and sparkling as with diamonds; it stretched away for about five miles to the great blue shadow, which the wall of rocks and ridge of snow in the north cast wide from the low-hanging sun. There was not a sound, not a breath of moving air; no bird came by; not an insect hummed. It was an hour of absolute stillness and perfect repose.

We tried to sleep, but in the bright sunshine no ghost of slumber would consent to visit the camp, till clouds at last came up which barred snow and sky across in grey and silver, robbing the shadows of their blue, and lowering the temperature to a comfortable degree. Then sleep descended, and coming late lingered with us all too long, so that it was noon of the 30th before we were again on the way. The snow was now soft and the apparent level proved, by the evidence of the sledges, to be a steady uphill slope. For an hour the pass kept its distance; then, on a sudden, it was near. Excitement rose. What should we see? What was beyond? We knew that the slope on the other side must be toward Ice Fjord, but that was all. The east coast of what I have named King James Land* is well seen from

* The first English explorers of Spitsbergen, Hudson and other servants of the Moscovy Company, formally took possession of the country on behalf of the King of England. They named it " King James, his New Land." This name has long been disused. Now that the interior of the island begins to be explored, names are needed for the different natural divisions of the country. I have therefore given the name of King James Land to the mountainous area included between Ice Fjord and Foreland Sound.

Advent Bay and other parts of Ice Fjord. It consists of the fronts of a series of big glaciers and of the ends of the mountain ranges dividing them. The glaciers and ranges are approximately parallel to one another, running from north-west to south-east. We therefore thought it probable that we should look down some glacier from the col, but doubted which. Arrived on the pass (2500 feet), there, in fact, was a glacier directly continuing the King's Highway down to the eastern waters, for it apparently ended in the fjord. Far off, and still in the same line, was the purple recess of Advent Bay. A beautiful row of peaks, pleasantly varied in form (for there were needles and snowy domes and pyramids among them), lined the glacier on either side, the last on both hands being bolder and more massive towers of rock than the rest. We afterward easily identified these peaks from Advent Bay, whence also on a clear morning I confirmed our observations by looking straight up this same glacier and recognising Highway Pass.

Camp was pitched on the pass and preparations made for a day's exploring in the neighbourhood. It was warm, the temperature in the tents being 59° Fahr., whilst the direct rays of sunshine really scorched. The condition of the snow may be imagined. Without ski, progress in any direction would have involved intolerable discomfort and labour. Close at hand on the north was a hill about 500 feet high, to which we gave the name Highway Dome. It was the obvious point to be ascended for a panoramic view. There was a *bergschrund* at the foot of it, and then a long snow slope up which we had to zigzag. Unfortunately by the time the summit had been gained the sun was obscured by clouds, which were boiling in the north as though for a thunderstorm. The hills of known position near Advent Bay were likewise obscured by cloud, so that my three-legged theodolite had made this ascent to little purpose, but the panorama was clear in the main and the colouring all the richer for the cloud-roof.

We were standing at an altitude of about 3000 feet,* surrounded by peaks of similar, or rather greater, elevation. Let no one fancy that because these heights are insignificant there was any corresponding insignificance in the view. The effect produced by mountains depends not upon their altitude, but upon their form, colour, and grouping. There are no features in a mountain, standing wholly above the snowline, whereby its absolute magnitude can be estimated by mere inspection. You may judge of its relative magnitude compared with its neighbours, but of its absolute magnitude you can only judge when you have acquired

* I cannot give the exact altitude, because Nielsen, who was carrying the instruments, dropped the aneroid here and smashed it before I had registered the reading.

experience of the district. A native of the Himalayas coming to the Alps would see them double their true size. A Swiss would halve the Himalayas. A slope of stone *débris* is the best guide to eye measurement, because stones break up into small fragments everywhere; but in these high arctic regions, far within the glaciers, there are no such slopes. It is only the multitude of mountains seen in any extended panorama of Spitsbergen that suggests the smallness of the individual peaks; but this very multitude is itself impressive. To the south, for instance, we looked across at least five parallel ridges; and there were indications of others beyond, a very tumult and throng of hills, none of which could we identify. The opposite direction interested us more at the moment, for our idea was that we might find there a route round to the Three Crowns. There was, in fact, a large *névé* basin, but so intricately crevassed as to be practically impassable in fog. One way was discoverable through the labyrinth, and apparently one only. The weather looked so threatening that we incontinently decided against making the attempt. This *névé* was one of several that fed the next big glacier to the north, which empties into the sea at Ekman Bay. Beyond it came a chaos of peaks; we learned to know them by sight well enough a few days later. The waters of Ekman Bay were in view, and the depression containing Dickson Bay could be traced, then the wall-fronted mass of the Thordsen Peninsula, and, far off, the high snow plateau, where we had wandered in the fog a few days before. Looking back the way we had come, we saw Kings Bay apparently very far off, much farther than Ice Fjord, which seemed, comparatively speaking, to lie at our feet. Differences of atmospheric transparency had some share in producing this effect.

A cold wind diminished our pleasure on the summit and shortened our stay. The descent presented problems to inexperienced skisters. The snow-slope dropped vertically from the summit crest for a yard or so, and was then very steep. Svensen, an expert on ski, tried to shoot down, but came a cropper before reaching the gentler incline. We, of course, fell headlong in hopeless fashion, and all attempts at glissading failed. Where the slope began to ease off a little a start was finally made, and a long curving shoot of about a mile carried us with exhilarating swiftness down to camp. Later on in the day the ascent was repeated, but with no useful result, for clouds still masked the important points of reference in the panorama. Excursions were also made in other directions, and a plan decided on for the morrow. Clouds kept forming, but only to fade again; by evening the weather was satisfactorily re-established. The play of shadow on the wide glacial expanse was inexpressibly lovely. Under full sunshine any very large *névé* appears a mere uniform sheet of white, admirable for brilliuncy but lacking in detail. When shadows come, the undulation of the surface is disclosed by long curves—infinitely delicate and fine in form. Of course, however bright the sun, there must really be a difference in the intensity of the light reflected at different points owing to variations of slope, but this difference is slight, and the eye, astonished by the brilliancy of sunshine upon snow, is not conscious of it. But when a cloud comes over the sun and casts a broad shadow on the *névé*, the varying illumination of the bending field becomes readily perceptible, though still faint and of marvellous delicacy, and a new order of beauty is revealed. He would be but a starved lover of mountain beauty whose eyes should desire to behold the regions of snow always beneath a cloudless heaven.

CHAPTER VI

OSBORNE GLACIER AND PRETENDER PASS

EXPLORERS in most parts of the world are able to sketch general maps of large areas, which they may have traversed only along a single line of route. Undulating country intersected by prominent waterways and rising at considerable intervals to prominent altitudes can be mapped in a sketchy fashion by the rapidest traveller, if skilled. A few compass bearings fix the position of prominent points; positions, astronomically determined from time to time as opportunity arises, clamp the whole together and enable it to be adjusted on the proper part of the globe; whilst, as for details, who cares about them in a new country? The mountain explorer, however, that person most unpopular with geographers, is faced by topographical problems of a far more complicated character. His routes always lie along valleys, whose sides cut off the distant view and whose bends often prevent him from looking either ahead or back. When he climbs a peak, assuming him to have a clear view, which is rare, he beholds a wide panorama, it is true, but, save in the foreground, it consists of a throng of peaks, whose summits alone are visible over intervening ridges. If, following tradition, he laboriously fixes the position of some of them, it is lost labour, for the mere dotting upon a map of the points of a lot of peaks tells a geographer nothing. What he wants to know is the number and direction of ranges, the position of watersheds, the relation of rivers to the original earth-crinkles which determined their direction and in turn are so remarkably modified by them. To make merely a sketch-map of a considerable mountain area thus involves an amount of travel within it beyond all comparison greater than that entailed by the exploration of open country. The smaller the scale of the mountains, and the closer they are packed together, the more frequently must the area be traversed in different directions before a sketch-map of it can be made.

King James Land is an example of a region excessively difficult to map. It is covered by a wonderful multitude of mountains, which may be described in a general way as planted in ranges running from north-west to south-east. Of these there are about six principal ones between the King's Highway and the Dead Man, and quantities more to the north. The old-fashioned geographer would have been content to draw parallel caterpillars on his map and so fill it up. But, as a matter of fact, there are throngs of subsidiary ranges and crossing hollows, so that the glacier, flowing down one valley, robs from its neighbour the snow accumulated in its upper reservoir; and it is exactly in these phenomena that the geographical interest of the region consists, for they show how ice-denudation works, and the kind of modelling effect which ice can produce on a land surface, an effect totally different in kind from that fabled by home-staying geologists, with their imagined excavating ice-streams.

Thus far we had only made acquaintance with one glacier-valley cutting across the island from Kings Bay to Ice Fjord. We determined to look into another, to the south, before turning northward to the Crowns group. On July 31 we accordingly broke up camp, loaded the sledges, and bade the men set off, down the way we had come, as far as Junction Point, where they were to await our arrival. Garwood and I, in the meantime, were to cross the range of hills at the south of our camp, descend into the next valley, and return over the pass at its head, which must of course give access to the snowfield of the southern branch of Highway Glacier. Descending that we should come to Junction Point.

It was another brilliant day, and so warm that the snow was softened to an unusual depth. During or immediately after frost the surface of *névé* sparkles in sunlight as though sprinkled with countless diamonds; but on warm days there are no diamonds, but only drops of water, the surface crystals being melted. The forms and surfaces of snow are thereby softened, and this softening effect is recognisable even from great distances. At starting, the view over Ice Fjord was clearer than ever, and we could distinguish Bunting Bluff, Fox Peak, and other scenes of last year's toils and delights. The work immediately in hand was to ascend a long snowslope, rising from Highway Pass to a col about 200 feet higher in the range to the south— a broad snow-saddle at the foot of a very fine peak, the ascent of which from this side would be dangerous, for its whole face is swept by ice-avalanches. Somewhere in the rocks of this peak are the nesting-places of many birds, the chorus of whose voices was heard as a faint hum. The new pass looked down upon the head of a large glacier, and across it to an innumerable multitude of peaks, all shining in the blaze of midday. At our feet was a secluded bay of this glacier. A splendid ski-glissade landed us on its snowy floor, and we were soon out on the main glacier, which swept down from the pass we were to cross next. Halting at a convenient spot, we took stock of the view. It was beautiful, of course—every view is beautiful in King James Land; but its interest made me forget its beauty for a time. We expected to find in this trough a glacier parallel to the Highway, and we did find one, and a large one too, larger than the Highway, because fed by several tributaries from the south; but to our surprise this glacier did not flow in the expected direction, but due south for many miles, and instead of ending in Ice Fjord, or on its shore, ran up against a big mass of mountains and, bending round to the right or south-west, disappeared from view. At the angle it received a wide tributary from the north-east. This great glacier, in fact, empties itself into the head of St. John's Bay. As that bay was originally named Osborne's Inlet, after an early whaling skipper, we gave his name to this glacier. Garwood, I believe, explains the twist of the mountains which cause this deflection of the glacier as the result of a fault dying out; but, lest I should unwillingly misrepresent his conclusions, I leave him to describe them himself. The mountains near at hand to the south were of beautiful forms, reminding us of well-known Swiss peaks, Weisshorns, Gabelhorns, and so forth. There was much aqueous vapour in the air, reducing its transparency and adding to the effects of distance. The mottled sky cast a decorative patchwork of shadows on the snow. Skeins of cloud were forming, and in the north the weather was again threatening dark and evil things.

On us, however, toiling up the long, long slopes to the pass, coy as are all the wide white passes in this land, the sun shone with painful fierceness. It burned as it sometimes does on the high Alps, so that we soon began to suffer from sun-headaches and parching thirst. Nowhere was there a drop of water to be squeezed from the apparently sodden snow. Having survey instruments and cameras to carry, we were sparely provided with food. Hunger came to weaken us and double the apparent length of the way. At last we were on the col, but the downward slope was very gentle and the snow now became sticky, so that the ski would not slide. We bore away to the right in search of a steeper incline and struck blue ice covered with mere slush that even the ski sank into. There were dry patches of it, too slippery to stand on; it was a mere alternation of evils. Sometimes we stuck fast and sometimes fell heavily. What was looked forward to as an easy and delightful excursion became a most laborious day's work. "This is your picnic," cried Garwood to me as he fell more than usually hard, "I hope you like it." But all things come to an end, and so did this march. Junction Point appeared in sight, with a lake-basin between the branch glaciers where they join, a basin similar to that at the foot of the Terrier, and, like it, recently drained. The heavy ice, formed on its surface in the winter, had been carried all over the neighbourhood by the momentum of the escaping water, and now lay spread about, high and dry.

With a struggle and a scramble we passed round the head of the lake and came in view of the men resting on the sledges. The unbelieving Svensen had climbed a neighbouring eminence to look out. Nielsen informed us that Svensen had been full of forebodings all day. They would never see us again, he said. We were gone into the wilderness and would be engulfed; as for them, when the provisions were finished they in their turn would die of starvation. Fool that he was not to take his old woman's advice and stay at home where he was well off, instead of coming to this snow-buried circle of the infernal regions! Camp was pitched on the very tracks of our upward journey. Then the sky clouded over and the wind rose. After one last look towards Kings Bay, reflecting the golden west and framed by purple hills, we closed the tent-doors and rejoiced to be "at home."

The lovely weather re-established itself in the daylit night, so that, when we awoke, sunshine lay abroad upon the glacier. Looking downward we had on our right hand the dull slope of the Queens group, where a smooth side glacier comes slanting down the midst of it from a col whose existence had not been revealed till now. It was decided to climb to this col for the purpose of making a closer investigation of the structure of the group. The march accordingly began with a long traversing descent of the main glacier to a point on its right bank at the foot of the side glacier. It mischanced that the area to be traversed was exactly the wettest belt of the whole basin. We skirted it on the ascent; now we had to go right across it, and that too after a series of fine melting days. The watery surface shone like a lake, and did in fact consist of a succession of pools, communicating with one another by slushy belts through which streams sluggishly meandered. The reader must not conceive of the pools, streams, and snow as corresponding to water and land, for the snow, even where it emerged, was permeated with water like a saturated sponge. When the autumnal frost masters a snowbog and binds its errant molecules into a mass, there is formed a solid, built up of ice-prisms, each about one inch in diameter and as long as the bog was deep. Prismatic ice of this kind, the product of the preceding winter, is frequently met with on Spitsbergen glaciers. Its cause puzzled us greatly when first we came upon it. With the motion of the glacier, the formation of crevasses, and so forth, it often happens that the side pressure which held the prisms together is removed. Their tendency is to thaw and separate along their planes of junction. By this means are produced opening sheaves of long ice-crystals, most beautiful to look upon. I have found them in quantities a foot or more long, opening out " like quills upon a fretful porcupine." Where there is no relaxation

WATERLOGGED SNOW

of lateral pressure, the crystals are held together; but they form a fabric of weak cohesion, and when you tread upon it your foot crunches in, almost as far as into snow.

Across this uncomfortable region we travelled for hours. Sometimes there were deep channels to cross; rarely a dry, hard patch intervened; most of the time there was slush of different consistencies which we had to push through. The sledges seemed to grow heavier and more resistent every hour. One of them, of which the runners were not shod with metal, came to grief at a stream-gully, where it pitched on its nose and smashed a runner. At last the water was left behind and dry ice gained. At the foot of a long, downward slope we found a big, frozen lake that had not yet burst the bonds imposed on it by the previous winter; crossing its rough surface, we climbed on to the moraine beyond, at the foot of the side glacier now to be ascended. The stone *débris* of dolomite rock, covering the lower part of the slope, were dotted about with various common plants, *Dryas octapetala*, *Saxifraga oppositifolia*, arctic poppy, and so forth, the same that grow in the interior wherever there is any soil to accommodate them. Of the ascent little need be said. We shall not soon forget it. The slope was the steepest encountered by the sledges. Our forces just sufficed to raise them, but there was nothing to spare. We arrived at the level top exhausted. Camp was pitched on the col, a wide snow-saddle between the Queen (4060 ft.) and an unimportant but commanding buttress peak. To the latter I hurried, desirous of making observations while the view was clear, for sea-mists had been observed crawling up both from Kings and English bays, and uniting on the pass near Mount Nielsen. There is nothing more beautiful than a sea-fog beheld from above when the sun shines upon it. By contrast its brilliant metallic whiteness makes purest snow grey. Then it moves so beautifully, gliding inland and putting out arms before it or casting off islands that wander away at their own sweet will. Enchanting to look upon are these sea-fairies, save to the victim to their embraces. Once inveigled, all their beauty vanishes, for within they are cold, cheerless, and grey, like the depths whence they spring. But to-day they were not destined to advance far. They came up boldly a while, then faltered and turned back, remaining thenceforward among the seracs and crevasses, except a few rambling outliers that floated away over the glacier or hovered as bright islands in hollows of the surface. Faint beds of variously transparent vapour, horizontally stratified, barred across the fine range of craggy mountains and their glacier cascades that filled the space between Cross Bay and the Crowns Glacier, a mountain group with an exceptionally fine skyline. We were encamped at that level of the glacier which may be described as the singing level, where water trickles all about, tinkling in tiny ice-cracks, rippling in rivulets, roaring in *moulins*, and humming in the faint base of the remoter torrents. It is only on slopes of a reasonable inclination that these sounds arise. The flat snowbogs of our morning traverse were soundless.

Late in the evening, the weather being perfectly re-established, I returned alone to camp. It was an enchanted hour. On one hand, as I sat in the tent-door, facing the sunshine and the view, was the fine peak we named Pretender, rising above the battlement-ridge of the western Queen. On the other hand was a lower hill, shutting off the distance and turning toward me a splendid precipice of rock. Between them was the opening through which the glacier, falling away from my standpoint, joined the apparently boundless expanse of the Crowns Glacier. Beyond were beautiful hills with the silver mist kissing their feet, and, above them in the clear sky, a few wisps of cloud. No breath of air moved, but falling waters sang from near and far, and a fulmar's whirr occasionally broke the stillness. At such times Nature gathers a man into herself, transforming his self-consciousness into a consciousness of her. All the forms and colours of the landscape sink into his heart like the expression of a great personality, whereof he himself is a portion. Ceasing to think, while Nature addresses him through every sense, he receives direct impressions from her. In this kind of *nirvana* the passage of time is forgotten, and as near an approach to bliss is experienced as this world is capable of supplying.

The passing hours, whereof some were devoted to sleep, witnessed the establishment of the weather's perfection. Heights and depths were cloudlessly clear, save low down over the bay, where the bright mist stretched like a carpet far out to sea. Buckling on my snowshoes, I slid forth down the slope, which curved over so steeply at the top that its foot was hidden by the bulge. The exhilaration of that rush through the crisp air is yet quick in remembrance. The cliffs on either hand, glorious battlemented walls of dolomite, seemed to be growing as we descended the side-glacier, whose exit, when we came to it, proved to be closed across by a rampart of moraine. Over this moraine, at a later hour, the sledges had to be carried to the ice of the extreme left margin of the Crowns Glacier, up which we were now to advance. There was no threat of serious impediment for a mile or so, but unexpected obstacles always lie in wait —the seasoning salt of the delight of exploration. A hundred yards on we were brought up sharply by a deep, impassable ice-gully or water-channel, stretching away into the glacier on the left and

PRETENDER CAMP 107

coming out of the moraine. We turned along its bank and came into the angle where an equally impassable tributary channel branched into it. There was nothing to be done but follow this backward to an overhanging place, cross it there, and then carry the sledges in turn, about a quarter of a mile over moraine, to a point where the other channel fortunately proved traversable. Hummocky ice succeeded for the rest of the march, beneath the grand cliffs of the Pretender (3480 ft.). Two great corries cut into these cliffs, the second of them starting exactly beneath the summit of the peak. We camped at a safe distance below its narrow mouth, beyond the range of frequent volleys of falling stones.

From this point to the base camp would be one long day's march for men with sledges. We had three and a half days' provisions left. We could therefore only spare two and a half days for exploration of the neighbourhood. That was not enough, so we sent the two men away with empty sacks to fetch more stores. There was plenty of work to be done in the neighbourhood, for the Pretender's cliff disclosed all the mysteries of the great fault, which, cutting right across the country, approximately along the line of the King's Highway, divides the uncontorted, almost horizontally stratified plateau-region of the north from the series of ranges of splintered peaks extending southward to the Dead Man. Accurate observation and careful mapping were, therefore, essential.

After lunch, when the men were gone away, we sat on a sledge in the sunshine, with our coats off, rejoicing in life. The glacier was working and cracking about us unceasingly; stones kept toppling from the moraine close by. High aloft rose the Pretender's cliff, 2000 feet, almost sheer. It is the most beautifully coloured cliff I ever saw. For foundations it has a contorted mass of ruddy archæan rocks, brilliantly adorned with splashes of golden lichen, picked out with grass-grown ledges. Here, as all along the mountain's face, are the nesting-places of countless birds. The fulmar petrels choose the lower edges; some, as we found, only just beyond reach of a man's hand. The wall below them is generally overhanging, for the birds know exactly the limits of a fox's climbing powers, and they avoid places accessible to him. Higher up are the homes of the little auks, who sit close together in rows, sunning their white bosoms. On the top of every jutting pinnacle of rock a glaucous gull keeps watch, with his own nest near at hand, ready to dive into any unprotected nest, or to pounce on any unfortunate bird that falls a victim to disease. The little auks always fly together in companies, I suppose for mutual protection. There is continual warfare between them and the gulls, but it seems to be carried on in accordance

NESTING BIRDS

with some accepted law, for though any stray auklet or fallen fledgling is fair game for a gull, he does not seem to attack individual auks sitting near their nests. Indeed, we often saw auks and glaucous gulls sitting close together on the same ledge, when it would have been easy for the gull to have snapped up one of his small neighbours. This, however, must be illegal. We never saw such a crime committed, and the auks evidently felt confident of the gull's correct behaviour. The nests are not placed in the gullies where stones habitually fall. No matter how big stone-avalanches may come down the usual ruts, the birds watch them unconcerned. But when a stray stone fell down the cliff in an exceptional direction, the birds flew out in their hundreds and thousands, filling the air with protests, the fulmars swooping around, the little auks darting forth horizontally at a higher level straight out and back again, whilst the glaucous gulls more leisurely floated away on confident wing, their white plumage seeming scarcely more solid than the glowing air which sustained their poise.

Above the ancient foundation rocks of the mountain comes a bed of green sandstone, above this a dark red bed, the same which forms the substance of all the Crowns group, except their caps. On the top of the sandstone, whose face has a sloping profile, is planted the summit cap of pink dolomite, cut off on this side in a plumb-vertical cliff horizontally stratified. High aloft in the wonderful air this rose-pink cliff, with its level lines of orange and other tones, like courses of masonry, was an object of rarest beauty, as all who know the Dolomites of Tirol can realise; but the sharp clear atmosphere of the Alps must yield the palm to the soft mellow arctic air, in which Spitsbergen's mountains almost seem to float. Rose-pink aloft, then purple-red, then green, and finally red again splashed with orange and green : such was the chord of colour presented by this lovely mountain-face between the blue sky and the white glacier foreground.

A funnel-shaped gully, with its upper edge at the foot of the dolomite cliff and the foot of its couloir ending on the glacier, was exactly behind our camp. Snow-slopes at its head were melting fast in the sun, so that a cascade laughed aloud all down the height of it. Stones were continually loosened by the melting; each started others in its fall, so that the rattle of tumbling rocks, now and again swollen by the roar of some big stone avalanche, kept the air in ceaseless vibration.

I made two expeditions out upon the glacier in different directions for the purpose of investigating its character at its most energetic part, just below the summer snowline. It was a maze of crevasses throughout its entire breadth and all the way

GLACIER PHENOMENA

down from the edge of the *névé* to the sea. A few traversable lines of route could be found, either parallel to and between the crevasses, or across them, where, owing to a change of slope in the bed, the lips of the crevasses were brought together within striding range. At best the surface was very bumpy, and I foresaw a bad time coming for the sledges. The ice phenomena would have struck any Alpine climber as curious. Every year there are added, even to the central and crevassed portion of an arctic glacier, accumulations of ice formed by the thawing and re-freezing of the winter snow, and these patchwork additions take the most unexpected forms. For instance, a crevasse that happens to be full of water will be roofed over with ice a few feet thick. If the rest of the water is then drained off a tunnel is formed, across which again crevasses may open. We found two or three such tunnels, whose roofs had been squeezed up into barrel-vaults. One of them was still full of water, but the roof had been raised high above it by pressure, and a doorway had been formed by the fall of a portion of the arch. I climbed into this grotto and stood on a ledge. Sunlight glimmered through the crystal roof; the walls were white; for floor there were the indigo-blue depths of the water. This was but one of the strange and beautiful objects that the glacier offered to the wanderer's admiration. Near the foot of the Pretender a blood-red river, dyed with the dust of the falling sandstones, flowed in a deep white channel cut into the glacier. It soon came to the crevasse that was its fate and plunged down the fatal *moulin*. That was close to camp. Of course, we called it the Moulin Rouge!

After wandering far I returned home for the night, meeting Garwood on the way. Our backs were to the boundless snowfields; before us the Pretender's mighty cliff shone warm under the mellow midnight sun, pink high aloft, crimson and green at lower levels, and striped blood-red where the water was pouring down. The white-mounded glacier was mottled over with blue shadows. Perfect weather, perfect scenery, perfect health—what more could we desire?

CHAPTER VII

THE SPITSBERGEN DOLOMITES

WHEN the sun passed round behind the Pretender, casting his shadow out upon the glacier far beyond camp, a hard frost set in, sealing up the runlets of water and binding the loosened rocks on the face of the cliff, so that stonefalls became rare; but no sooner did the fiery monarch come out from his retreat behind the mountains in the east than all the batteries of the hills opened to salute him. The afternoon of August 3, being our morning, Garwood and I shouldered packs for a scramble on the Pretender, minded to pass northward round his foot and then make way up the ridge that forms, higher up, the lip of the funnel of the falling stones. The weather was glorious, but the white sea-fog had crept up to the tents, so that we set forth from the very edge of the mist. After going some little way up the main glacier we bore to the right on to the hillside, and went diagonally up a slope of snow. Below on the left was a *bergschrund*, and above on the right were the steep rocks. Presently the slope increased and became of hard ice, into which Garwood cut steps. The position was not altogether a safe one, for we had not bothered to bring a rope, and now discovered that quantities of stones were in the habit of falling down the slope into the *bergschrund*, which was ready to engulf either of us impartially in the event of a slip. However, we did not slip, and the sun had not yet reached the stones, which were still in the bondage of frost. The rocks above the slope were safely reached and a brief scramble carried us over the edge of the ridge on to the screes of the north-east face. Beyond them was a wide snow-slope reaching up to the steep dolomite cap that forms the top 500 feet of the peak. The snow was hard frozen, so the ascent had to be made up the screes. They were particularly loose, and that is all to say about them. Scree-slopes are never anything but nasty to climb. The top of them was the edge of the nearly level ridge, whence we looked down into the funnel on the other side and across to the beautiful dolomite cliff visible from camp. At the foot of the *couloir* of the funnel we could just discover our tiny tents.

The point thus gained was all that could be desired for surveying and geologising. Now was displayed in all its wide extent the *névé* region of the Crowns Glacier, utterly different in character from that of the King's Highway. Here was no ice-filled trough between two serrated walls, but a huge expanse, so gently sloping as to appear flat—a marble pavement, of three hundred square miles, beneath the blue dome of heaven. Far away it swelled into low white domes, on whose sides a few rocks appeared, whilst in the north-east was its undulating upper edge, beyond which were remoter snow-covered plateaus with mountain summits peering over from yet farther off. The white *névé* was lined by the many-branching water-channels of its drainage system, like the veins in a leaf, indicating the structure and trend of the ice. Where areas were crevassed, blue shadows toned the white. Everywhere the delicate modelling of the surface, by slightly varying the amount of light reflected to the eye, produced a tender play of tones, within the narrowest conceivable limits from brightest to darkest. The whole was visibly a flowing stream, not a stagnant accumulation, for the curves of flow were everywhere discernible. Thus a sense of weight and volume was added to the effect of boundless expanse which first overwhelmed the observers. The noble flood of ice, narrowing considerably between the hill on which we stood, and the beautifully composed group of sharp-crested rock-peaks opposite, disappeared beneath the floor of sea-mist whereon the sunshine lay dazzling.

Turning round toward the east from this enthralling prospect, the eye rested on the group of the famous Crowns. They are called the Three Crowns on all the maps, but there are many more than three. The prominent trio are pyramidal hills of purple sandstone, shaped with almost artful regularity, each surmounted by a cap of the same dolomite limestone as that which crowns the Pretender. They resemble golden crowns above purple robes. The caps are the fragmentary remains of an ancient plateau, denuded away in the lapse of time. Just behind the Three Crowns we saw a low broad pass, giving access to the head of a glacier flowing eastward. There was sea-fog lying on it also, so we knew that Ekman Bay could not be very far off in that direction. This is the lowest and shortest pass between Kings Bay and Ice Fjord. Lightly laden men could cross this way in a long day's march from sea to sea, climbing one of the Crowns *en route*. The expedition would take them through what is, to my thinking, the finest scenery in Spitsbergen. The whole panorama was clear to the remotest edge of the horizon, flooded with undimmed sunshine, and overarched by a sky faintly blue below, deeply azure in the fathomless zenith.

We spent some hours at this point, lunching admiring, and taking observations. The view was, to me, so novel in character, so beautiful, so full of revelations that, for a long time, I was too excited to work. The other side, though less

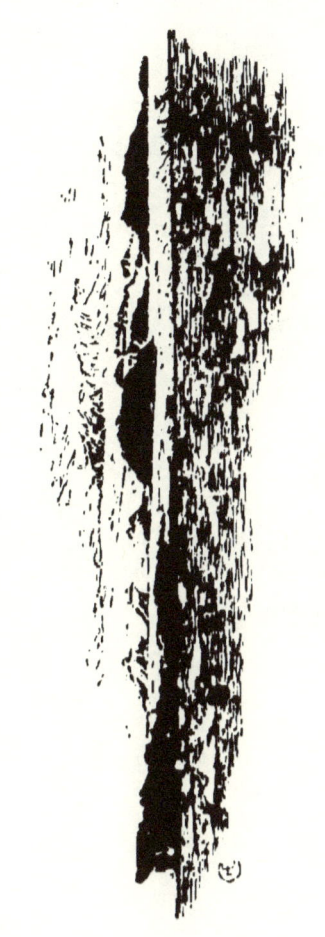

THE THREE CROWNS FROM KINGS BAY.

unusual, was hardly less wonderful. There the eye plunged down into the depth of the funnel, and beheld the stone-avalanches beginning their fall. Far below were the flocks of birds flying about the rocks. Their cries came faintly up to us. Finally, close at hand there was the great dolomite cliff, an absolute wall, more than ever resembling some artificial structure, the work of giants, falling to decay. The varied colouring of its beds and the vertical streaks caused by trickling water were as beautiful close at hand as when seen from the depths of the gulf of air below. We walked along the narrow ridge to the actual foot of this cliff, where the *arête* rises vertically, so that the further ascent must be made by the north-east face. There was a height of about 500 feet to be climbed by way of snow slopes, here and there narrowing into gullies between protruding beds of rock—so, at least, we thought, but the attempt showed that the slopes were of hard ice. The step-cutting involved had no attractions, for there was nothing to be gained by ascending to the peak. It would only show, on the other side, country already known to us, whilst we were to have many better opportunities of looking northward from points both higher and better situated. What settled the matter finally was the sight of our men just arriving at camp heavily laden with good things. We accordingly turned round and took the easy way downhill, glissading a good part of it on treacherous snow-covered ice.

After supper another expedition was made down the glacier all along under the Pretender's face, in further investigation of the fault. It is only thus, by constant moving about beneath a great cliff, that one is finally enabled to realise its magnitude. One true measure of scale that a healthy man possesses is fatigue. When you have learned by actual experience that it takes several days' marching to pass the base of a big Himalayan mountain, you begin to feel the size of the thing. A precipice of 200 feet differs only in size from one of 2000 feet. To appreciate the majesty of the larger, you must become physically conscious of its scale. Such knowledge has to be laboriously acquired. No one, I imagine, who has not climbed the Matterhorn, can have any real conception of the magnitude of the pyramid beheld in the view from the Riffel; yet a consciousness of the magnitude is an essential element in the impressiveness of the view. I believe that only mountain climbers are in a position to thrill with perfect resonance to the glory of a mountain prospect. The passion for mountain-climbing derives much of its power over men from thus fostering and developing in them the capacity for admiration, wonder, and worship in the presence of Nature's magnificence.

Next day (August 4) camp was again struck

ASCENT OF THE MIDDLE CROWN

for an onward march, some supplies being left behind for use on the way down. The crevassed nature of the glacier involved the choice of a very devious route far out upon the ice, then back toward the Crowns. When the foot of the middle Crown was reached, I called for my camera, but it could not be found. It had dropped off Nielsen's sledge, and he must go back to retrieve it. Garwood and I accordingly set off to climb the Crown, leaving Svensen below, plunged again in miseries and forebodings, now that the sea was becoming remote and snowfields were spreading their hateful expanse around him. The pyramids of the south and middle Crowns are planted together on a snowy plinth. Up the slope of this we ascended on ski, taking a devious course to avoid the steepest incline, at the same time steering clear of a few groups of open crevasses. In three-quarters of an hour we were standing at the foot of the rocks, where the ski were left behind. A long and steep slope of *débris* had next to be surmounted. The material lies in an unstable condition and slips away beneath the foot at every step. Keeping as close as possible to the left *arête*, we gained height steadily. The *débris* accumulation becomes thinner as the summit is approached. Halfway up, little walls of rock emerge, and afford some agreeable scrambling. By the last of these the *arête* itself is gained and the ascent completed along it, except where an overhanging snow cornice forces the climber down on the south face. A little chimney gives access to the crowning rock (4000 ft.). The ascent from the top of the snow-slope took three-quarters of an hour. It is easy enough. The southern Crown (3840 ft.) can be similarly climbed by its south face, but the northern Crown (4020 ft.) would be more difficult, for it is cut off, apparently all the way round, by a short precipice, perhaps a hundred feet high. There are some gullies grooved into this wall, but they too are vertical. One or other of them would certainly prove climbable if any one cared to give the time needed for the attempt. All three Crowns were reputed inaccessible by the general opinion of persons who had only seen them from Kings Bay.

Our ascent was made for the purpose of obtaining a view, and generously were we rewarded. The northern Crown is higher than the middle one, and that in turn than the southern; but the differences are a few feet only, whilst in point of situation the middle Crown is best placed for a panorama. Garwood and I agreed that it was the most beautiful we had seen in Spitsbergen, though it was afterwards equalled by the view from the Diadem, and surpassed, in some respects, by that from Mount Hedgehog. What struck us most was the colour. The desert of snow was bluish or purplish-grey; only the sea-mist, hiding

VIEW FROM THE MIDDLE CROWN 121

Kings Bay and the foot of the glacier, was pure white. In the foreground were the golden Crowns above purple slopes casting rich blue shadows. On the snowfields lay many sapphire-blue lakes. All the rock in sight was of some rich colour—yellow, orange, purple, red. Large glaciers radiated away in several directions : one down to Ekman Bay, whose head we could see, another to Ice Fjord, beyond whose distant waters we recognised Advent Bay and the hills behind it, with clouds lying still upon them. Last year, whenever we saw King James Land in the distance the sun was always shining on it. This year the Advent Vale region was hardly ever seen clear of clouds. It is the bad weather, as King James Land is the fine weather region of Spitsbergen.

To the south were a maze and multitude of peaks. We thought that we identified Hornsunds Tind in a solitary white tower very far away. I afterward took a true bearing of it with the theodolite, and, on reducing the observation at home, find that the peak observed stands exactly in the line of Hornsunds Tind ; so that if the two are not identical the coincidence is extraordinary. The distance of the mountain from the Three Crowns is just a hundred miles. I find it difficult to believe that such a distance can often be pierced by the sight in the relatively dense atmosphere of Spitsbergen. Foreland Sound was, as usual, full of fog, but the peaks of the Foreland itself rose out of its shining embrace. The highest group is south of the middle of the island; its members are beautifully white and of graceful form. Farther north the peaks are smaller and only their tips appeared. The Cross Bay Mountains with their serrated edge looked finer than ever; then came the great snow-field, beheld in all its extent, stretching up to a high undulating crest and back to remote bays and hollows—fascinating to look upon, but who shall say how wearisome to wander over? Far away to the north-east was a row of mountains of varied forms, some white and dome-like, others sharply pointed, others again chisel-edged. We saw them now for the first time, and believed them to be the range that borders Wijde Bay on the west; but they have since proved to be the mountains at the head of that bay, between it and Dicksons, a range of unsuspected importance in the structure of the country. The sky overhead was blue and clear, fading downward into white, as in an old Flemish picture. There was no movement in the cool air. Garwood left me alone on the top and went down to crack rocks. Long did I sit in perfection of enjoyment, letting my eye roam round and round the amazing panorama. There was a peculiar sensation of being in the midst of a strange world, whose parts seemed to radiate from this point. Never did I feel more keenly the wonder of the domain of ice. Utter silence reigned, till there came a writhing in the air, heard but not felt. It passed, returned, and passed again, as though flocks of invisible beings were hurrying by on powerful wings.

Chilled to the bone, at length I began the descent, picking up Garwood and some of his fossil spoils on the way. A magnificent ski-slide carried us in a great curving zigzag, first to the foot of the southern Crown, then round the snowy base to the tents. We dropped a thousand feet in a few minutes. So keen was the joy of this rush through the air, that we talked of scrambling up again to repeat it, but the attractions of supper proved more powerful than those of glissading.

Our view from the middle Crown showed that nothing was to be gained by pushing camp farther north, unless we went very much farther than the means at our disposal permitted. The whole region for many miles round could be mapped from the summits of hills within reach of our present camp. We judged it better, therefore, to climb from that base, rather than to spend time dragging sledges about over almost featureless snowfields. So, next morning (August 5), away we went on ski—Garwood, Nielsen, and I—carrying instruments and food on our backs, and delighted to have no hindering load a-drag behind. The weather continued faultless. Our plan was to follow the left margin of the glacier to the bay beyond the northern Crown, to turn up that to its head, and to climb the Diadem Peak, whose situation seemed specially favourable for a view. The snow was very soft and became softer every hour, but we shuffled comfortably over it and pitied our poor colleagues in the Alps, wading knee-deep in *névé*. The surface was not really in good condition for skiing; it was too soft and adhesive to be slippery. However, we made good progress, and in less than two hours the northern Crown was passed and the side glacier opened. It flows down from a ring of dolomite-capped peaks and comes out into the main glacier between the northern Crown and the peak beyond it, named by us the Exile because its crown has been wholly denuded away. It is a regular pyramid of red sandstone with top and corners rounded off. There is not a fragment of rock visible *in situ*, the whole solid substance of the mountain being buried beneath accumulations of *débris*.

Turning, then, with the northern Crown on our right hand, the Exile on our left, and the great snowfield at our backs, we made diagonally up the side glacier toward a snow-saddle between the Exile and the Diadem. All the snow was saturated with water, which gravitated to the middle of the valley and formed a great Slough of Despond there. Advancing very gingerly to find a way across, I suddenly sank up to my waist in the freezing mixture. The ski turned round under my feet and fastened them down, so that I was helplessly anchored, and it was all that Nielsen and Garwood could do to withdraw me from the uncomfortable position. We ultimately passed round the head of the Slough and swiftly made for the rocks of the Exile, where I undressed and wrung out my dripping things. Whether it was more comfortable to sit half-clothed while the things dried, or to put them on in a sodden condition, was a question I am now enabled to decide by experience. Fortunately the sunshine had a little warmth in it, but the preliminary bath certainly did not add to the enjoyment of lunch.

Just below the rocks was an open *bergschrund* into which Nielsen tumbled, ski and all, but he caught the upper edge and extricated himself with a mighty kick and pull. The hidden crevasses over which we slid were countless, but the ski deprived them of all power to injure or annoy. A slide from the rocks to the broad snow-saddle, then the ascent of the Diadem began. We knew that it would present no difficulties below the summit rocks. They were vertical on our side, but there were indications that the snow-slope reached far up them on the other. For some distance we could climb straight ahead ; then the slope steepened and we had to zigzag, each man choosing his own route. About six hundred feet below the top, ski could no further go, for the surface was hard frozen, so that they obtained no grip upon it. They were accordingly left behind, planted erect, for if they are left lying down they will assuredly find means to break loose and go careering away to some remote level place. As soon as it became a question of kicking steps in the increasingly hard and steep slope, the scattered elements of the party concentrated and so came to the foot of the final peak together. A snow-slope, as we had foreseen, reached almost to the top, but it was cut across by two large *bergschrunds*, well enough bridged. The rope was now put on and the final approaches made in orthodox fashion. Scrambling up a few steep rocks, we came out on the curious little flat summit plain (4154 ft.), from whose edges the drop is vertical all round, except where the slope we ascended abuts.

The view resembled that from the middle Crown, but was more extensive to the north and east. The whole island was displayed. We overlooked the region of almost horizontally-bedded, chocolate-coloured sandstone, capped with dolomite near at hand, but dipping away from the old rocks underlying it, which appeared in the north-east as mountain ranges. Advent Bay was again clearly visible across Ice Fjord, so that the Diadem and the Crowns can be seen from the hotel there, a fact previously unsuspected. I set up the instruments and worked for more than an hour, growing colder and colder in the raw air. Garwood and Nielsen warmed themselves by building a big cairn as a monument of our climb.

The first stage of the descent required some care, for the slope was steep and of ice, whilst the bridges over the *bergschrunds* did not appear particularly strong. Once on the main snow-slope the rope could be laid aside and each could make for his ski by the shortest route. Nielsen went on ahead and disappeared over the bulging declivity at a great rate, but when I tried to follow his example I found it difficult to maintain a footing on the hard, icy slope. The boards under my feet shot away so quickly that without a powerful break I could not maintain my balance. No application of the spike of the ice-axe to the slope produced friction enough to prevent the bewilderment of a lightning-like descent, which always ended in a shattering overthrow. How Nielsen had managed remained a mystery to me, till I came up with him and learnt that he had put his ice-axe between his legs and sat upon it, thus turning himself into a tripod on runners. Riding, like a witch on a broomstick, he gained the gentler slope below without delay or misfortune. Garwood was less lucky, for one of his ski gave him the slip and raced away on its own account. We heard him howling aloft, but knew not what about till his truant shoe had dashed past, heading for a number of open crevasses. It leapt these in fine style, but bending away to the right, made for the hollow, north of the Exile, to which we had to descend to fetch it. Rather than reascend and return over the mile of snow-slope down which the ski had shot, we changed the route of our return. To see Garwood walking about unroped among the maze of crevasses and crossing *bergschrunds* by rotten snow-bridges was decidedly unpleasant. If he had fallen through anywhere we could have done nothing for him, and he would never have been seen again ; but the fates were propitious. Instead of sliding down as we did, he had to wade through knee-deep snow, but that was the limit of his misfortune.

The great snowfield was joined at the north foot of the Exile, and straight running made for camp. It was a long and thirsty shuffle back, for, since my immersion, we had come across no drop of drinkable water, all that flows from the Exile and the northern Crown being chocolate-coloured and thick with sand. Areas of snow formation, new to us in appearance, were passed below the Exile ; the most remarkable was where the surface of the *névé* was covered with a kind of scaly armour-plating, consisting of discs or flakes of ice, hard-frozen together, piled up and projecting over one another. Wind was the determining agent, I fancy, in producing this phenomenon. Steadily plodding on over the now uneven and adhesive snow, at last we reached camp, about midnight, well satisfied with the expedition. We had travelled eighteen and a half miles over the softest *névé* snow imaginable, besides climbing our peak and devoting some hours, *en route* and on the top, to the work of surveying. Without ski this would have been hard work for three days. During our absence Svensen had cleaned out the tents, dried and aired our things, and otherwise made himself useful. He had never expected us to appear again, so that his work was perhaps the more meritorious. Late at night we heard him lying in his tent and " prophesying " (as we used to call it) in deep and solemn tones to Nielsen. The further we went from the coast the more frequent and solemn were these deliverances, not a word of which could we understand. I asked Nielsen what they were about. "Oh," he said, "he talks about his farm and his old woman, and what she gives him to eat; and then he says if he ever gets back home he will not go away any more as long as he lives."

A few hours later Svensen set forth on his ski to fetch an instrument I required from the baggage below the Pretender. He was instructed on no account to quit the tracks made by the sledges on the way up, and to take care not to fall into any of the crevasses. Once fairly alone on the glacier, he proceeded to set these directions at naught. The tracks were devious; he would make a short cut and save himself time and distance. What mattered the maze of concealed crevasses? He frankly walked *along* them, whether on their arched roofs or the ice beside them being a mere matter of chance. We saw his tracks next day and wondered at his many escapes. As it was, he fell into two crevasses and only extricated himself with much difficulty. The Svensen that returned to camp was a yet sadder and more pessimistic individual than the one that set forth. He had looked Death in the face, and seemed to feel swindled in that he had escaped destruction.

This day the sky was actually covered with an unmistakable heat haze. Thunderstorms, I believe, never occur in Spitsbergen; if we had not known this, we should have thought one was brewing. It was actually hot and stuffy within the tent, but outside the temperature was perfect. Our intention was to climb the middle Crown again, when Svensen returned, and to spend some hours on the mountain, Garwood photographing and hunting for fossils in the limestone, I observing angles. At last we could set forth with theodolite and whole-plate camera for the top of the Crown. There was no novelty in the ascent, except that the sky was steadily clouding over, so that we had to race the weather. Unfortunately the clouds won. The sun was blotted out when we reached the top, many hills were obscured by clouds, and the panorama was rendered relatively uninteresting. There was nothing for Garwood to photograph, and far fewer points for me to observe than I could have wished. The cold became bitter. Fiddling with the little screws of the theodolite was horribly painful. I endured it for more than an hour before complete numbness rendered further work of that kind impossible. Nielsen kept warmth in his veins by prizing crags away; they thundered and crashed over the precipice on the north, finding a swift descent down one of the many vertical chimneys, and then rushing out on the snow-slope beneath. The results of his labours were widely spread abroad below. Before packing up to descend we all joined in building a big cairn, which, I think, will last for many years. A hurried descent down rocks and screes and a fine ski-slide to camp set the blood circulating merrily in our veins. The tents were just within the margin of a fog, which hung like a veil over the western landscape, where a mottled roof of cloud above the jagged crest of the Cross Bay hills shone golden bright, fading away below into the misty grey foreground of vaguely-outlined, broken ice.

CHAPTER VIII

RETURN TO KINGS BAY

ALL appearances were convincing that the weather had finally broken up, but a charm seemed to lie upon King James Land this year, for next morning (August 7) was fine as ever, with skies brilliantly clear. The white fog still covered the bay and the glacier's foot, but retreated before us as we advanced on the downward journey, for which the time had now come. Instead of going far out on to the glacier, as in our ascent, we kept a more direct course, for crevasses that are too wide to drag sledges over when going uphill are passable on the way down. The sledges had to make many a downward jump, and were greatly strained, but we reckoned they would hold out to the coast, and so let them take their luck. It was none of the best. A certain broad crevasse opposed to our advance its yawning chasm, whose higher side was much above the lower. The first sledge took the jump safely, but the second landed heavily on its nose, and one runner snapped in half. We tied it up with string, but the jagged edge greatly increased the friction during the remainder of the journey. Near the Pretender we re-entered the circuit of the nesting birds, and found their feathers at every step of the way. A solitary fulmar sitting on the ice only stirred when we approached him within two yards. Then he flapped his wings and ran, gradually rising into the air and helping himself up by beating the ground with his feet, the action used by fulmars when they rise from water. He did not fly far, for he was obviously ill. Doubtless a glaucous gull presently put an end to his existence.

Having kept along the left side of the glacier, we came, at the foot of the Pretender, as we knew we must, to a steep ice staircase, a slope of about 200 feet, broken by a series of large crevasses. A longitudinal fold in the ice, caused by the narrowing of the glacier at this point, added a more complex irregularity to the steplike descent. This was the worst place we had to convey sledges over on the glaciers of Spitsbergen; nor shall I attempt to describe our labours. The sledges were slung across some crevasses, let down over others, gingerly conducted along ridges of ice narrower than themselves, with profound chasms on each side, hauled round the flanks of seracs, and otherwise forced forward as circumstances decreed. Once only did a misfortune occur, and then the fault was mine. The slope was very steep, and there was a crevasse in the way. Nielsen got on to its lower lip and began lifting the bow of the sledge forward by means of the drag-rope. I was hanging on behind with the pick-end of the ice-axe hitched into the stern. Just at the critical moment something gave way. The ice-axe slipped out; I fell backwards; the sledge lumbered down. That it would go right into the crevasse and be utterly lost seemed certain. But no! it merely turned a somersault and wedged itself in between two projecting noses of ice, which held it firmly, till, with the assistance of the others, we brought it safe to land. Shortly afterward the site of Pretender Camp was reached, and our little heap of stores found undisturbed by foxes or birds.

We knew that the most tiresome part of the day's journey was yet to come; the lunch-halt was consequently prolonged. To the foot of Pretender Pass the way was easy enough, but beyond that point difficulties were bound to accumulate, for the glacier became so crevassed as to be impassable even for men without sledges, whilst, instead of snow-slopes along the left bank, there was a widening lateral moraine. Fortunately we found an irregular belt of snow between the ridge of this moraine and the *débris*-slope behind it; along that belt we were able to make intermittent advance, though the snow was freely strewn with blocks of stone, over and around which, up and down and in and out, the sledges had to be lifted and dragged. We were thankful even for this small mercy, seeing that, if the snow had not been there, we must have raised the sledges bodily and carried them more than a mile over the nastiest kind of moraine. As it was, we had to carry them for several short spells. How easy it looks on paper! Four men, one at each corner of the sledge; they lift her, and along she goes. But in practice, when the ground to be traversed consists of loose rocks, each about the size of a man's head, with ice below them, sloping this way and that, uphill two yards, downhill three yards, now tilted to the right, now to the left, some one is always stumbling. They jog one another from side to side. The weight gets bandied about and heaved in all directions, so that each wastes most of his work in counter-balancing the unintentional irregularities of his fellows' efforts. A halt had to be made halfway along, but we vowed to finish this horrible part of the route before camping. The stove was lit and cocoa brewed to put heart into the men; then on again, plunging, tripping, twisting ankles, barking shins, till at last there came a practicable though lumpy stretch of ice alongside the moraine, and we could launch the sledges on it and haul them forward with less toil. We were close to the angle where Kings and Highway glaciers join, and the lateral moraines of both, uniting at the promontory of the dividing mountain, flow out as a medial moraine, and are carried on by the glacier and ultimately dumped over the ice-cliff into Kings Bay. We crossed this medial moraine at the earliest convenient place, then followed along beside it till near midnight, when somebody, turning round to survey the view, found it beautiful, and proposed that camp should be pitched straightway.

The air was crisp and cold. The sun shone golden in the north, just tinged with the first promise of its winter setting. The mellow light flooded with unusual glory of colour the many-tinted rocks of the Crowns and Pretender, grouped together in fine assemblage between the two great glaciers, now both at once beheld back to their highest snowfields. Such purples as the autumnal midnight sun pours out on the so-called Liefde-Bay sandstones of Spitzbergen had no rival even in the richest product of Tyrian skill. All night long the glacier worked and cracked beneath us in its onward flow, squeezing its slow way down through the narrowing channel. Loud reports disturbed our slumbers, and at an early hour brought us back to consciousness of the beauty of the world and the continuing loveliness of the weather.

The sky remained clear, and the white fog brooded over the waters of the bay, when the men started down with the sledges, leaving us to sit awhile on convenient rocks, smoking and enjoying the splendid scenery. Presently we also set forth, not down, but across Highway Glacier to examine the rocks of its left bank. A very large lake-basin had to be crossed at the margin of the ice. It proved to have been drained by the biggest ice-tunnel I ever saw, a cavern at least fifty feet in diameter and more than a hundred yards long. I bolted into it, under the stones perched loosely on its brow, and took some photographs of the weird grotto, whilst Garwood climbed the riskily loose cliff behind and hunted for fossils. Keeping across the mouth of a minor side glacier, we came to the moraine crossed by us with so much trouble on the upward way. The great hollow beyond it was now perceived to be another and yet larger lake-basin, drained in its turn by the ice-cañon which had formed one of our first considerable impediments. This lake-basin is more than half a mile in length, and some hundreds of yards wide. It lies at the foot of Mount Nielsen. Here, losing sight of Garwood, I turned to seek the sledges. Not finding them, and being too cold to loiter about, I walked briskly on down the foot of the glacier, and did not halt till the base camp was reached. It remained just as we left it, thank goodness! But it must have had a narrow escape, for, at some time during our absence, a flood of water came down the fan on which it stood, cutting a new channel, whose still wet margin ran less than a hand's breadth from the angle of the tent. Had the channel been deflected a couple of yards, all our goods would have gone to sea !

The roof of fog was overhead, yet the view was most beautiful, for the sun shone through holes in it upon the glacier's terminal cliff, barring it with vertical bands of light and colour. There were stripes of purple, violet, green, blue, and white, made by the staining of the ice with stone *débris*, or by new fractures manifesting the varying transparency of the mass, or by the play of light and shadow upon it. The jagged hills looked down through holes or behind veils of mist. The water was absolutely calm, but more thickly covered with broken ice than when we last beheld it ; in fact, over great areas, the floating blocks seemed to form a continuous ice-covering. In calm weather this mattered little, but if a northerly wind set in, all the ice would be driven and packed down upon us, and we should be imprisoned, who could say for how long ? Obviously, therefore, it would be our business to shift camp as soon as possible to some more favourable situation.

Long I sat in the tent-door gazing at the view and dreaming. What changes had taken place here since Professor Sven Lovén's visit in 1837, the first visit of any man of science to this part of Spitsbergen ! The island of which he wrote so fully, with its " diminutive Alps" and moraines, was separated from the glacier at that time by a channel of open water 1000 feet wide; now the glacier almost surrounds it and has buried out of sight the ground on which he stood. It had already done so before Nordenskiöld's visit in 1861, since when no considerable changes have taken place. This is only one of many instances of glacial advance during the present century. A comparison between the seventeenth and eighteenth century Dutch charts and the maps of the present day proves the general truth of this observation. The development seems to be still in progress. Witness the great glacier-front which has descended into Agardh Bay since 1871, and over which we went in crossing the Ivory Gate last year. Glaciers which end in shallow waters must, indeed, be advancing slowly as they fill up the bay heads, but this does not suffice to explain so great an advance as that of the Kings Glacier between 1837 and 1861.

The arriving sledges, dragged by men soaking with perspiration, stopped these meditations. Both sledges were on the point of breaking up, such had been the strain upon them during the last fortnight. They were extra strongly built, and the runners were protected with metal sheaths, yet there was not a sound joint left in them. The metal had all been scraped and torn away, the runners smashed up. If ordinary arctic travel were as rough as this work over crevassed inland glaciers, such a sledging expedition as Nansen made from the *Fram* would be impossible, for no sledge could hold out a tenth part of his course. Our sledges, moreover, were lightly laden with about a third of the normal arctic load. Had they been heavier, they could not have been dragged along at all, or if forced forward they would have broken up the first day.

It is only on returning to the coast that one obtains a correct realisation of the silence of the higher regions. The glacier-front kept " calving "; the floating ice kept cracking up and turning over; there was a noisy torrent flooding down close to camp. Stones fell; waves broke on the shore. Such noises for a long time drove sleep away. When I did slumber it was to dream of glacier-lakes bursting, of avalanches falling, and other catastrophes.

Next day we had the boat to drag down to the sea—two hours' work—all our baggage to overhaul, pack, and portage, so that it was late in the afternoon before we were ready to sail. The long hours of work were enlivened by the charm of the scenery beneath the grey roof of sea-fog, which still remained just where it had hung for so many days. The variety of effects was extraordinary, for there was no wind to move the fog, nor sunshine coming through it. The floating ice sometimes stood out white against the purple background and dark sky, sometimes dark against a white curtain of mist, and sometimes it glittered behind a vaporous veil. The water was now dark, like lead, now bright as burnished steel. There was continual change, yet no visible cause for change. Out into this fairy region of calm water and pure ice at last we rowed in search of new scenes, new beauty, and new delights.

Our first goal was one of Lovén's Islands, away out in the midst of the bay, right over against the ice-cliff of the Kings Glacier. To reach this we had to row through a bed of water so closely covered with broken ice that a way was made for the boat by pushing the fragments asunder. They were of all sizes and colours. Surfaces that had been exposed to the air for some time were white, as all ice becomes under such conditions. Others newly cloven, or that had formed till recently the submerged face of floating blocks, were blue or green. There were pink pieces, dusted over with sandstone *débris;* but the majority of the small blocks, and most were small, were crystal clear, like lumps of purest glass. The water was absolutely still. Sunshine lay upon it, and the great glacier-cliff, along which we rowed, was reflected from the watery mirror. Every few minutes the glacier "calved," and the resulting waves rattled the ice about us, whilst the booming thunder came echoing back from remote hollows of the hills. Nielsen was reminded of days spent by him as a sailor in fogs on the Newfoundland banks, when, as he said, they used to smell the icebergs long before they loomed into view. Kings Bay, of course, presents no bergs comparable in size to those that drift southward down the coast of Greenland, though the floating masses we were soon to approach were much larger than those ordinarily met with in Spitsbergen waters. As our distance from the south shore of the bay increased, the mountains behind it were better seen, and proved to be a fine ridge with many peaks, the watershed between Kings and English bays. A series of glaciers descend in their hollows, but none reach the sea, for there is a broad belt of flat land all along the southern shore. The view up Kings Glacier now became of entrancing beauty as the fog cleared away, and all our peaks from Mount Nielsen round to the Diadem were disclosed. How different was this view to our eyes, which recognised every feature and knew what was behind every impediment, from our first outlook there last year, in a brief interval between two storms ! The culmination of the charm came when the small, partly ice-covered island rose into our foreground, and the surging waves of splintered glacier thrown up behind it contrasted with the smooth wide-spreading snowfields far beyond. The ice-cliff north of the island was more shattered than any we had yet beheld. Here the greatest floating bergs enter the sea. They do not fall into it, but simply float away,

LOVÉN ISLANDS

being already quite detached from one another by the deep clefts of the ice.

From an examination of a great many sea-fronting glacier-sections we learnt that crevasses, however long and wide, seldom penetrate very far down into the mass of ice. I do not remember ever to have seen any crevasse (except at this point) which cut a glacier-cliff down to sea-level. Higher up in the *névé* region crevasses may be more profound, but towards a glacier's snout I am sure that their depth is often greatly overestimated. The ice in the foundation of a glacier exists under great pressure and behaves very differently from the surface ice, which is free to break up under lateral strain. A careful study of arctic ice-cliffs would, I think, give rise to several unexpected revelations. The opening up of Spitsbergen to ordinary summer travellers would enable such simple but illuminating researches to be undertaken by holiday-making men of science.

The archipelago, which I have named Lovén's Islands, after the explorer who first recorded a visit to them, was now close at hand. We made for a convenient cove and landed. Countless screaming terns saluted us with a chorus of unmistakable imprecations. No bird that ever I saw can swear like a tern. Till it opens its mouth you would think it the very incarnation of gentleness and grace, such the purity of its white plumage, the slenderness of its form, and the elegance of all its motions. But it is my matured conviction that in every tern there resides the spirit of a departed bargee. On these islands Lovén found countless nesting birds of many sorts, besides the spoor of reindeer and foxes. We found only eider-ducks, terns, and a very few geese; of reindeer not a trace. There are no reindeer left on the west coast of Spitsbergen. We never saw a footprint on the shores of Klaas Billen Bay, Kings Bay, or Horn Sound this year, though in all three bays are square miles of country admirably suited to feed and maintain them and once supporting large herds. The ruthless Norwegian hunter has exterminated them utterly.

I need not expatiate on the gorgeousness of the view from these islands. It was especially fine to the north where white icebergs of all fantastic forms floated in the dark purple reflections of the hills. The only sound heard, besides the screaming of the terns and the boom of the glacier-cliff, was the innumerable ploppings of water against the myriad floating blocks of ice. We landed on another island to cook a meal and survey. The little plants were putting on their autumnal colourings, most of the birds-nests were abandoned, the young broods—alas! sadly few in numbers—disporting themselves in the neighbouring waters. All the islands are smoothed by ice, for the Kings Glacier was once at least 500 feet thicker and very much longer than now. Probably, there are other mounds of rock, continuing under the glacier the line of these islands, and rumpling up the ice into a crevassed condition otherwise difficult to account for.

Turning away from the islands, we rowed toward the east end of the rounded hill standing out into the fjord, to which we gave the name Blomstrand's Mound. From the published account of the Swedish Expedition of 1861, we were led to expect that Scoresby's Grotto would be found in this direction. It was only afterwards, when we procured a copy in the original Swedish, to which are appended maps, not reproduced in the German translation, that we discovered the whereabouts of this grotto in Blomstrand's Harbour.* We now had to wind about amongst large floating towers and castles of ice, entrancingly beautiful. The number of the great floating bergs seemed countless. We passed by devious ways along channels, between them, often being so entirely surrounded as to seem on a lake built all about with ice-castles. Some were hollowed out into caverns with walls thin enough to let the light of the low hanging midnight sun shine through.

* It is greatly to be regretted that no scale is attached to these six maps of harbours, which cannot therefore be applied with certainty to any general map of Spitsbergen.

We manœuvred to get one of these directly between us and the sun, so as to enjoy the resplendence of its opalescent shimmer, contrasted with the blueness of the shadowed side of the ice. Deep in the substance of the crystalline wall shone out a host of sparkling points like many-faceted diamonds enclosed in cloudy crystal. The evening was perfect : calm, bright, mellow, clear to the remotest distance, save just at one point where a sea-mist came pouring over a pass from English Bay, with a rainbow mantling on its shoulder.

The drowsily creaking oars at length brought us to the mainland, where camp was quickly pitched on soft ground near a brook. There was no grotto anywhere in the neighbourhood. The slope of Blomstrand's Mound rose temptingly behind. With plane-table and camera we hastened forth to gain a more commanding panorama. About 500 feet up was a convenient knoll, whence the upper part of the mound was displayed as an undulating plateau bending away to the culminating dome of the hill over a couple of miles of bog land and broken rocks, extraordinarily disagreeable to walk upon. The whole mound is encircled on three sides by the bay, whilst on the fourth a large glacier descending from the north abuts against it, and sends an arm down into the sea on either side. The view was, of course, most extensive and beheld under rarely favour-

COAL HAVEN

able conditions, for the low-striking, golden sunlight mellowed all the glaciers and the hills. The bay spread abroad below, as in a map, and the icebergs on its surface were tiny dots of white, whilst the areas closely covered with smaller, broken ice resembled surfaces crisped by some gentle breeze.

At 4 A.M. (August 10) we turned in. A few hours later the weather was still fine, but at noon the Crowns began to put on caps of cloud. Mists gathered in all directions, wind rose, and soon all was overcast and rain was falling on the tent. The spell of fine weather was, in fact, at an end. By 3 o'clock we were rowing away in water no longer calm. Yet it was charming to watch the graceful rocking of the smaller pieces of floating ice, and to see them turn over as their equilibrium was disturbed. The old white surface went under, the new blue side came up. There was now but one day left before the *Kvik* ought to call for us. The weather was too thick for surveying, so we settled to make at once for Coal Haven, where tertiary fossil plants had been found, though not the characteristic *Taxodium*.* Accordingly we rowed straight across the bay, though no sign could be seen of any inlet such as the chart marks. There is, in fact, no inlet at all, but only a low headland that protects the anchorage from

* Garwood was fortunate enough to discover a fine specimen of this.

westerly winds. It is completely open to north and east. On reaching the south coast and finding no trace of the expected inlet, we rowed along the shore toward Quade Hook for a couple of miles. It was an open, pebbly beach, on which we might have hauled up the boat, but whence it could not have been launched in face of any sea, like that now threatening to rise. Leaving the men to keep the boat off shore, Garwood and I landed to prospect. Just behind the narrow beach was a low cliff, the front of a wide area of boggy and stony ground from which the hills rise, half a mile or so inland. Westward was no bay whatever, so we concluded that Coal Haven lay to the east, where, in fact, we presently discovered it, behind a low spit of shingle a few yards wide, enclosing a lagoon.

While the men pitched camp, Garwood and I walked inland to look for the coal-bed. Its position is carefully described by Lamont, but we had only the book on the Swedish expedition of 1861 with us, and, though the members of that party visited and, I believe, discovered the coal, they give no accurate account of its position. We dimly remembered that it was found where a glacier-stream cuts a section into the ground. There were two glaciers ending about a mile inland from the bay, so we walked towards them and tracked up every stream flowing from them, but found no coal. I then went to the west, Garwood to the east, till every inch of land within Coal Haven had been traversed. It was no good. A big stone man planted on a mound, and with a slanting stick built into it, seemed likely to be a guide to the hidden treasure; but there was no coal in the mound, nor anywhere in the direction to which the stick pointed. We have since learnt that the cairn marks one of the points whose position was astronomically fixed by the Swedes,[*] and that it has nothing to do with the coal, which in fact is not found within Coal Haven at all, but within the next bay to the east, where of course we did not look for it.

A low cloud-roof, intermittently dropping rain, hung continuously over Coal Haven during our visit. Only the bases of hills and the grey snouts of glaciers emerged beneath it. Sometimes a dense mist came up; rarely the drizzle held off for half an hour. In this cheerless case black melancholy invaded Svensen. At a moment of gloomy forgetfulness he filled the pot with sea-water for brewing soup. The mistake was fortunately discovered in time, for there was no food to spare. When Garwood returned with half a dozen guillemots, the last shot-cartridge had been fired off. Svensen skinned the birds for the pot with the sadness of a man condemned to death.

[*] The position as determined by the Swedes does not agree with the position determined by the Austrians.—*Vide* R. von Barry, *Zwei Fahrten*, &c. Vienna, 1894. 8vo.

"We will only eat half of them to-night," he said. "Why?" I asked. "Because this is the last proper food we shall have, and we may as well make it hold out as long as possible. When did you say the *Kvik* is coming for us?" "At midnight to-night," I answered. "Not a bit of it. *Ikke!* I heard the sailors on the boat say the captain would not come for us at all. We shall starve here." "Skittles! They'll come for us to-day or to-morrow." "*Ikke!* they'll not come at all, I believe." "I tell you they will; the captain undertook to come." "*Ikke, ikke!*" We finished all the birds, but the food almost stuck in Svensen's throat.

When supper was done (it was the morning of the 11th) a surprising vigour seized our gloomy companion. He jumped into the boat, pitched its mast, sail, and some spars on shore, and carried them away to the point. We watched him build a big stone-heap and plant the mast in it with the sail suspended as a flag. Then he turned in and was heard loudly and solemnly prophesying to himself in his fine declamatory style. We breakfasted late in the afternoon on one of our last soups and some mouldy biscuits fried in the scrapings of the butter-pot; then we began to look out for the *Kvik*. The mouth of Kings Bay was not visible from camp, so we went for walks to various higher points, besides spending some hours over another hunt for coal; but neither coal

RUSSIAN TRAPPERS

nor *Kvik* appeared. The drizzling night dragged its slow hours along. A meagre supper in the morning of the 12th was the occasion of more loud lamentations from our Norwegian Jeremiah. The others then turned in, whilst I went off to the ruins of an old Russian hut on the neighbouring cape to watch for the expected steamer.

Less than a century ago there was a big winter settlement of Russian trappers in and about Kings Bay. As in the case of other Russian settlements, there were a central house and a number of outlying huts widely scattered from one another. The central house of this group was in Cross Bay, in Ebeltoft's Haven, I believe. The Coal Haven hut was only an outlyer, inhabited by a solitary individual, who at stated intervals visited the central depôt to leave his catch of furs and renew his meagre stock of provisions. Numbers of these trappers annually died of scurvy. The rock on which I sat had assuredly been witness to such unrecorded tragedies. There now remains nothing but the ground plan of the hut, with a few bits of mouldering wood and broken brick lying about. There were fragments of both Dutch and Russian bricks, as is not uncommon on these sites, for the Russians used the remains of older Dutch whaling "cookeries" in building their stoves. Against a big rock was a piece of stone wall and a rotting beam, apparently part of an old store-cupboard. Moss had crept up over it, and little arctic flowers were growing upon it with unwonted luxuriance. The bones of foxes and bears were in the ground, which was pervaded with corrupting wood-fibre and carpeted with a peculiarly rank moss that only grows thus luxuriantly on the abandoned sites of human habitation. What a desolate place for a winter dwelling, planted between a bog and the icy bay! Who lived here? I asked myself. What did he think about? Were the hills anything to him— the Three Crowns and those other peaks rising all around? Did the beauty of the long sunset heralding the arctic night find recognition in his eyes? Or was life too hard for the growth in him of any sense of beauty? Was he some poor creature forced as a last resource to come here for the bare means of subsistence, or some criminal forcibly expatriated to these inhospitable shores? Such indeed was the custom in Northern Russia before Siberia came into fashion as a place of exile. Long I sat, musing on these things in the grey night, and listening to the far-off rumble of the calving glacier. Every few minutes I scanned the sea horizon off Mitra Hook, and always thought I could trace the faint appearance of a remote steamer's smoke. Imagination is a dreadful trickster, but time always shows up its character. No steamer came in sight, though the appointed hour had passed. My watch completed,

THE KVIK

I returned to camp and sent up Nielsen to look out. "They haven't come," said Svensen, "and they won't come. *Ikke, ikke!* We shall never get away from here." This croaking raven of a man began to grate upon our nerves.

In the afternoon all turned out again. No signs of the *Kvik*. We assured one another that it was of no consequence. A fire was lit, the pot set on to boil and all our remaining provisions turned into it. If this was to be our last meal it should be as big a one as we could provide. Slowly the water came to the boil, all of us anxiously and greedily watching. Nielsen wandered forlornly off to the point. "The *Kvik*, the *Kvik!*" he shouted. "*Ikke, ikke!*" said Svensen, but no one heeded him; this time there was no mistake. Before our last food was swallowed she had rounded into the bay and cast anchor close by us.

CHAPTER IX

KINGS BAY TO HORN SOUND

ON boarding the *Kvik* we were again in contact with the outside world. There was much to hear and something to tell, so that time passed quickly. Baron Bornemisza, returning from a week's cruise in Wijde Bay and along the north coast, was full of information about the condition of the ice in that direction. It was not so open as at the same time in the preceding year. Hinloopen Strait was blocked about halfway down; the *Kvik* had been unable to reach the Seven Islands. At Advent Bay we found the more boldly navigated *Expres*, with our friend Herr Meissenbach on board, in a happy and triumphant state of mind. He had had the best kind of time, and enjoyed himself vastly, spending three weeks in the neighbourhood of the Seven Islands, and pushing as far east as Cape Platen. Two bears had fallen to the rifles of the party, and I know not how many seals; now he was on his way home.

That was a busy day at Advent Point, and a blustery withal, for the autumnal bad weather was setting in. All our baggage had to be packed for transfer to the *Lofoten,* in which we were to sail for Horn Sound that evening. At the inn were two Swiss artists and Professor Wiesner of Vienna, come to take observations on the intensity of the light. Presently a tourist steamer arrived and carried the artists away. People were coming and going all the time ; it was the culmination of the tourist season.

I have read in the London press that Spitsbergen, nowadays, is " overrun " with tourists. This is far from being the case. A considerable number come up with the *Lofoten* and other tourist ships, and pay a brief visit to the west coast, but few of them ever land except for an hour or two at Advent Point. Apart from Herr Andrée's party, the only visitors who spent any time in Spitsbergen this year were Baron Bornamisza and a few people who made trips on the *Kvik*, the German party who hired the *Expres*, and ourselves. Besides Garwood and me, only Baron Bornamisza and the artists made any attempt to go into the interior. The Baron spent two or three days with one of our tents in the Sassendal, shooting reindeer ; whilst the artists dragged a little sledge a day's journey into the hills west of Advent Bay, and camped there for a couple of nights. So much for the overrunning of Spitsbergen. The simple fact is that to spend any time in the interior of the island is no easier now than it was fifty years ago, nor is there much probability that it will become easier in the immediate future. All of Spitsbergen that the ordinary tourist needs to see is visible from the deck of a ship, whence it can be beheld without either labour or discomfort. To penetrate the heart of Spitsbergen glaciers now involves just the same kind of work that the crossing of North-East Land demanded of Nordenskiöld in 1873.

When the hour came for the *Lofoten* to sail, such was the boisterousness of the embarkation that some intending passengers preferred to stay behind for a week rather than be soused. The disturbing wind was only a local draught, such as often blows down the boggy valleys of Spitsbergen, and especially down the Advent Vale. When we were out in the midst of Ice Fjord the gale diminished to an ordinary breeze, by which we were well rolled all night long off the west coast. It was past noon (August 14) when the *Lofoten* turned into Horn Sound; she steamed straight up the bay and finally came to off the mouth of a small bay in the south coast, the Goose Haven of the old whalers. Our whaleboat was hoisted overboard, and such goods as we needed for a week lowered into it. Svensen, who was to be left on board, eagerly helping, and joyous to see the last of the hated sledges. He said good-bye to us with monstrous enthusiasm, mixed in apologies for not having enjoyed our company more keenly. If we would come to his home and go a-fishing with him he assured us that we should find no more active or willing companion.

The exchange from the warmth and solidity of the steamer to the rawness of the foggy day and the unrest of the tumbling sea was, to say the least, undesirable. Our friends on board watched our departure without envy, and it must be confessed that we rowed away with little eagerness. Clouds hung low and heavy upon the hills, and no scene could have been more desolate. In half an hour we landed on the stony beach of the east shore of Goose Haven; the *Lofoten* was then small in the distance and just rounding out of sight. There was no novelty of the unknown now ahead of us. We had come to make the ascent of Mount Hedgehog or Horn Sunds Tind, which Garwood had almost succeeded in accomplishing just twelve months before in company with Trevor-Battye and a seaman. The object of this repetition was to see the view from the top, a hope little likely to be fulfilled in such weather as was prevailing. Garwood also desired to investigate certain rocks, which he thought might prove interestingly fossiliferous. Save for these rocks I do not think we should have come to Horn Sound again. They proved to be a fraud, but that was not Garwood's fault. My own wish had been to spend our last week in Ekman and Dickson bays for the purpose of completing and joining my two maps; but I could hardly expect Garwood to be eager for such an arrangement, seeing that the area contained no geological novelties for him. My alternative proposition was that we should hire the *Kvik* and make a run for Wiches Land—the islands approached by us the preceding year, but never as yet landed on by any geologist. Unfortunately, we could learn nothing of the condition of the ice east of Spitsbergen, so hesitated to incur a considerable expense for a very problematical advantage. If only we had known! It was the one year of all recorded years in which the sea to the eastward was most free of ice, and, during these very days, Mr. Arnold Pike was steaming round and round and landing on the islands in question, where he shot fifty-seven bears.

For better or worse, we had decided on Horn Sound, and here we were by the resounding shore of Goose Haven. There was no good landing-place or protected creek for the boat. We had to land on the open beach. The baggage was pitched ashore and the boat completely emptied. Nevertheless, our reduced strength did not avail to haul it out of the water. We began to regret the loss of Svensen sooner than we expected. Camp having been pitched just above high-water line, there was nothing for us to do on the dreary shore, so we rowed across to the far point of the bay—Hofer Point—a convenient position for my survey. Garwood, knowing the way about, steered the boat into a tiny cove, whither we thought of transferring camp. The change was not made, fortunately, as will hereafter appear. At the head of the cove are ruins of a Russian settlement, on an exposed mound as usual, whilst on neighbouring knolls are two groups of graves. There remains also a bench in a protected corner. When the miserable life lived in these remote and solitary huts by most of the exiles is considered, these poor benches, of which I have now seen several examples, are peculiarly pathetic. Many a sad hour must successive, lonely, fur-clad watchmen have passed while seated upon them, marking the slow passage of miserable days. The sentiment of the melancholy landscape is strangely enhanced by a human interest of this kind, however remote. The savage regions of the earth are always impressive to a spectator's imagination, but they become infinitely more impressive when they can be regarded as a theatre of human suffering or endurance.

The others returned to camp by boat, whilst I pursued my task and wandered home round the bay's head, at first over sea-eaten rocks, afterwards, when the hills receded, over boggy land between the shelving beach and the iceflat at the foot of the great moraine of the glacier filling the bay's valley—the Goose Glacier, as we afterwards called it. On a mound of the bog are ruins of a cousiderable whalers' settlement, with quantities of great bones lying about, and the inevitable group of graves not far away. In the seventeenth century the Horn Sound whalers were English; in fact, this was one of the largest English settlements. The beach seems to have risen considerably since that time, for the whales used to be flensed between high and low water marks, whereas the bones now lie far beyond reach of the highest tides. It rained heavily as I walked on round the shore and waded the streams that flow out from the glacier. The clouds descended lower than ever, and the gloom, if possible, increased, so that the dreariness, by its very intensity becoming almost novel, became also indued with the pleasantness of novelty.

During our explorations of the previous year in the belt of boggy interior between Advent Bay and the east coast, every glacier we came across had an iceflat below its snout, formed by the freezing of the winter snow when impregnated by water drained out of the glacier. This year we had met with no examples of such iceflats before this one in Goose Haven. It was of great extent and evidently destined to survive the rapidly departing summer, for it still averaged about six feet in thickness. The glacier streams had cut deep channels through it, which the first heavy snowfall would easily block, again compelling the water to soak into the new bed of snow and

TORRENT IN A GLACIER ICE-FOOT.

GLACIAL ICE-FOOT

prepare it in its turn to be frozen solid later on. The intermittent thaws of spring may be more effective in forming the snow-bog, which is the needful preliminary condition of an ice-foot, than is the autumn drainage held back by the autumnal snowfall. As to this we possess no information. Between the two the phenomenon is produced. As a rule the summer thaw must suffice to melt the ice-foot away, for, if it did not, there would be a continual increase in the thickness of the ice, and a kind of glacier would be formed. Of such glaciers, however, we have seen no examples. Though we found several cases of ice-foot apparently destined to survive the summer, they probably owed their survival either to the fact that they were produced by exceptionally heavy local falls of snow, or to the summer's thaw being below the average in total amount. One year with another, the balance of formation and thaw appears to be equalised. At all events, we have no evidence yet of any glacial ice-foot that steadily increases. If, however, such an increasing ice-foot were to arise, it would tend to bury the terminal moraine and unite itself to the snout of the glacier, but before the process had advanced very far the surface of the ice-foot would begin to acquire a slope, on which a snow-bog could hardly be formed. The glacial water would be drained quickly away and the conditions for further increase of the ice-foot would no longer exist.

Considering such questions, I dawdled about on the beach and the ice, to the great disgust of some glaucous gulls, who kept swooping down close to my head with horrid cries. Rain falling heavily did not add perceptibly to the discomforts of the cold and blustery day. Near camp was another ruined whalers' settlement or cookery, surrounded by quantities of bleached and rotting bones, and with the inevitable grave-mound close by. The ruins in this case were better preserved, so that their character was recognisable. A whalers' cookery consisted essentially of two parts, a "tent" and a cauldron. The tent was a building of four low stone walls roofed with sailcloth passed over a ridge-pole and held down by rocks round the edges. The walls of the tent are still standing on a mound. Close by are the wrecks of the brickwork belonging to two cauldrons for boiling down blubber. Quantities of coal-slag showed the nature of the fuel employed. All about the ruins and amongst the bones, moss was growing with the peculiar rankness already mentioned as characteristic of the sites of human habitation in Spitsbergen.

Rain fell steadily all night long. The tide rising higher than before, banged our boat about, for all we could do was to drag it as high as the waves would carry it at high tide, and stand by to prevent accidents till the waters had retreated again. Obviously, we must seek some better haven.

Accordingly Garwood and I set forth along the shore northward to the point, and then eastward. Expecting no worse trouble than rivers to cross, I wore only rubber waders, and hands in pockets instead of carrying an ice-axe. This was all right so long as the beach lasted, but where cliffs took the place of beach, difficulties arose. The slope above the cliffs proved to be furrowed by couloirs filled with ice. Garwood being somewhere aloft, stone-breaking, I had to cross the gullies without assistance. This was accomplished by a new system. Having selected a couple of sharp-pointed stones, like palæolithic celts, I lay down and scrambled across, digging the stones in and using them as handhold. Fortunately the slope was not steep. In case of a slip I should have shot down the couloir fast enough, and been tossed out at the foot of it over the cliff into the sea. The point of the bay was reached beyond the fourth of these couloirs. The view over the head of Horn Sound was tolerably good, though the strong cold wind made its investigation anything but pleasant. The mountain-tops were hidden. It is their remarkably bold forms that make fair-weather views of the sound so beautiful. All the glaciers, however, were clear of fog. The end of the sound is filled by a very big one ; two others, descending from Horn Sunds Tind, jutted out the cliffs of their splintered sea-fronts between the end glacier and our point, whilst a whole series of minor glaciers descend to, or almost to, the sea, along the north shore, the principal one debouching into a fine bay almost opposite to us.

After taking observations at the point, I went eastward along the south shore, where, above a low rock wall, is a belt of fairly level ground intervening between the sound and a grand precipice that reached up into leaden clouds. A group of graves was passed, near the little rock-bound cove to which we afterwards moved camp. Half a mile on came a remarkable assemblage of great fallen rocks, looking from the distance like some ancient megalithic monument. The individual rocks were as big as houses; ages ago they all fell together in a mighty avalanche from the top of the neighbouring precipice. Almost all of them have been cloven in half by atmospheric denudation and frost, and the clefts afford delightful scrambles. In the midst of the ruin are mossy lawns, springs of clear water, a few pools, and accumulations of winter snow lingering in shady places. Here I came up with Garwood enjoying shelter from the wind in a quiet nook. The views from the tops of these rocks, and from various places among them, were most striking, especially when some glacier-front could be caught within a framing foreground of the splintered crags. We paid several visits to these Stonehenge rocks, as we named them. Garwood, I believe, climbed them all. Half a dozen contented me. Their quaintness grew upon

KITTIWAKE GLACIER

us. We were always finding new resemblances in their queer forms. Some had almost dissolved away, leaving mere pillars to represent what had been mighty cubes. One such pillar looked to me like an ancient Arabian bethel, but Garwood called it "a ripping tombstone"!

Some distance farther on came the first side glacier (Kittiwake Glacier), emerging, past the end of the precipice, out of a gap in the hills. Just at the angle is the resting-place of innumerable kittiwakes, whose cries mingled with the noise of the wind. The glacier was gained above its crevassed end, after a toilsome scramble up moraine. It proved to be snow-covered and full of hidden crevasses. Never, I suppose, was a glacier party less well provided than were we two men to face such conditions. My boots had slippery rubber soles; in each of Garwood's were just two nails. We had neither rope nor stick, our single implement being a small geological hammer. It may be imagined, therefore, that our further progress was made slowly and with much precaution. Ultimately we gained the middle of the glacier, and saw up it to the rocks of what afterwards proved to be Horn Sunds Tind disappearing into cloud. A few days later (19th) we returned better equipped, but in weather no wise improved. That time we crossed Kittiwake Glacier to its right bank, where are the red rocks which Garwood once hoped would prove to be

Devonian. They were an utter disappointment, and he turned from them in disgust. Beyond came a slope of screes, and then the next and smaller glacier, which likewise has a splintered sea-front, almost joining that of the great Horn Glacier at the head of the sound. We climbed on to a commanding hummock and gazed inland. Horn Glacier is wide and of gentle slope, with hills of small elevation immediately north of it as far as we could see. From the south it receives two or three considerable tributaries, divided from one another by mountain ranges of decided form, whose bases alone were disclosed. The island is here only about sixteen miles wide. My idea was to make a dash across and locate the position and direction of the watershed, which is probably near the east coast, but in such weather nothing could have been seen. A few miles inland fog rested on the snow.

The inner part of the sound and the north bay were dotted over with quantities of floating ice-blocks, fallen from various glacier-fronts, and steadily drifting out to sea with the tide. It was near midnight, and the sky was tinted with sunset tones just visible through thin places in the roof of cloud, as we returned to camp. Only hunger reconciled us to the sight of the tents, for the sea was rising with the tide, and at high water we must get afloat and move away to one of the more sheltered places round to the east beyond the point. Everything was duly packed, the boat loaded, and all was ready, but we could not get her afloat. Work as we might she would turn broadside to the waves, and nothing would keep her straight. Two oars were broken in the attempt. Then we unloaded her again and tried to get her off empty, but that was no easier. The weather was continually worsening, and our struggles became desperate; it was all wasted labour. A bigger wave than usual at last broke into and filled the boat, rendering her utterly unmanageable. There was nothing for it but to unpack everything and pitch camp again. The tide presently going down, the boat was once more left high and dry, so that at six in the morning we were able to turn in.

During the night Garwood was inspired with a new plan for hauling up the boat. To me it did not seem promising, but, as a matter of fact, it worked. Acting under his instructions, the three of us set our backs under the bows and shoved them transversely a few inches uphill, then under the stern and did the same. The double process moved her about one inch. It was repeated again and again. After two hours' work we had the satisfaction of seeing the boat well above high-water mark. But long before the time for high tide the waves, now grown large and thunderous, were almost up to her, and we had to go at her again as before and gain another few yards.

The weather was miserable. Clouds lay almost upon the water. When the tide turned we went for a walk inland to the foot of Goose Glacier and up its right bank, following the route by which in the previous year Garwood had approached the foot of Mount Hedgehog in exactly similar weather. We kept on up the glacier for some way, and the clouds became a little more broken as the distance from the sea increased. There even came a momentary hole in them, at the end of which a point of rock appeared with a stone man upon it. "There is the rock on which we camped last year," cried Garwood, "and there's the cairn we built." I only had time to identify it before the fog embraced and hid it once more. After that there was nothing to be seen. Rain fell, wind blew, and we turned homeward.

When the bay came in sight we perceived that conditions were not improved. There was no wind in Goose Haven itself, but a heavy swell was coming in from the open sea, breaking right over the rocks that make the little cove where we landed on Hofer Point, and tossing towers of spray into the air. I measured one of them by comparison with the cliff beside it, and found it to be fifty feet in height. A little anxious about our camp and boat, we hurried down and found them threatened by the inroading waves, already at half-tide reaching above the previous high-tide mark. The tents were quickly moved twenty yards farther inland. All the baggage was carried after them, and then came another turn at the boat, which was finally brought to a position of safety. Long before that was accomplished the place where the tents had been pitched was deeply covered by the boiling surf. Drenched with rain and generally disgusted, we turned in about the middle of the morning of the 17th.

CHAPTER X

ASCENT OF MOUNT HEDGEHOG

AFTER breakfast in the afternoon of August 17, as things looked a little better, we loaded ourselves with provisions, instruments, &c., and decided to make an expedition at all events to the base of Mount Hedgehog, and thence perhaps back to Horn Sound by way of Kittiwake Glacier. It was 8.30 P.M. when we set forth, all three in far from hopeful humour. We retraced the steps of the previous day, passing the ruined cookery, and going over undulating ground and up the right bank of Goose Glacier, then crossing the foot of a small side glacier, which brings down a moraine of grey marble streaked with pink, and so reaching the open ice where Garwood's cairn came into view. Last year hidden crevasses were troublesome hereabouts, but there was no such danger now. Crevasses were either open or covered with firm roofs of frozen snow. We roped, of course, but the rope was not required—fortunately not, for Nielsen disliked and distrusted it, and would not keep it tight, ultimately refusing to wear it any longer and preferring to go detached. Give him rocks or the sea, he said ; as for ice and snow he knew nothing about them, and did not feel safe on them, roped or unroped. Overhead was the usual roof of cloud. Gradually, as we advanced and left the coast behind, we perceived the roof was becoming thinner. Small holes began to appear, with faint suggestions of rock behind them. Our excitement increased, for Garwood knew that they were the rocks of Mount Hedgehog's great precipice. Thinner and thinner became the veil of mist as we walked expectant over the hard-frozen *névé*, the mountain behind becoming every moment more clearly disclosed, till at last it was fully revealed to us, a glorious wall of silver-dusted rock with the crimson fires of heaven falling like a mantle upon it. It was about midnight, two days before the sun's first setting. The radiant orb was upon the north horizon, half-buried in the fog above which we were rising. A flood of crimson light flowed from it over all mountains that rose above the clouds, so that every rock was like a glowing coal, whilst the snow-domes resembled silken cushions.

Now at length I realized the position and nature of that Horn Sunds Tind of which I had heard and read so much. It is not a peak, nor a mountain, but a range of peaks running, not parallel to Horn Sound, as marked on the chart, but at right-angles to it and almost north and south. At the north end of the range is the highest point, a needle of rock very similar to the Aiguille du Dru in form. This is separated by a deep depression from the larger, but, as we afterwards learnt, lower, mountain-mass to which we have attached the old name, Mount Hedgehog, originally given to the whole range by its English discoverers. Of this mass the culminating point is at its south end. From it there descends to the west a steep rock rib, ending below in a shattered little peak, beyond which comes a snow-saddle. The west ridge rises slightly again to a rock mound (Bastion Point), falls to another and wider snow-saddle, and is thence continued as a splintered rocky range, forming the left bank of the branch of Goose Glacier up which we had come. It was upon an outlier of Bastion Point that Garwood and his party encamped last year. We found their tent-platform as fresh as if it had only just been abandoned. Garwood affectionately identified the various empty tins lying about and was lucky enough to find his own pocket-compass uninjured where it had been forgotten. In the neighbouring cairn were the records of their climb, a separate one written by each member of the party.

There was no doubt in our minds what next thing demanded doing. We must climb the peak above, while the chance offered, for the sky overhead was brilliantly clear; there was no wind and

HORN SUNDS TINDER.

MERIDIAN ARC 173

no apparent change of weather impending. Sea, shore, lowlands, and glaciers were unfortunately buried beneath the floor of clouds, but all hills over 1000 feet high were likely to be disclosed, so that the view would be of great geographical interest. Nielsen preferred not to accompany our ascent, so we gave him the plane-table and whatever else could not be carried further. At 12.30 A.M. (August 18) we parted in opposite directions, Nielsen going back to camp, we two upward to the broad snow col between Bastion Point and the foot of the great west ridge.

Before describing the ascent it is advisable to show the rather special importance attaching to it. In the year 1823 Sir Edward (then Captain) Sabine was sent to Spitsbergen and East Greenland to make pendulum observations for determining the figure of the earth. From what he observed on that brief visit he was led to conclude that Spitsbergen is a land-area excellently adapted to the purpose of measuring an arc of the meridian in a high latitude, a measurement which would be of the utmost value for well-known scientific reasons not in this place needing discussion. It is enough here to say that Sabine set forth his ideas in a letter (February 8, 1826) addressed to Davies Gilbert, M.P., Vice-President of the Royal Society. From that day to this the proposal has not been lost sight of, but before an elaborately accurate measurement of a line some

240 miles in length could be undertaken it was necessary to decide upon the various points to be used for the angles of the trigonometrical net. This could only be done after Spitsbergen itself had been roughly surveyed. The first definite step toward carrying out Sabine's project was made by Professor Otto Torell,* who included in the plans of the Swedish Spitsbergen expedition of 1861 a reconnaissance of the meridian-arc. The work was to be divided between two ships, the *Æolus* and the *Magdalena*. Chydenius on the *Æolus* was to lay out the northern part of the line and select the points of observation from the Seven Islands down to the south end of Hinloopen Strait, whilst Dunér on the *Magdalena* was to complete the preparations down Wybe Jans Water to the South Cape. Owing to unfavourable ice conditions the work could not be wholly accomplished in that year. Another Swedish expedition was accordingly sent out in 1864, under Nordenskiöld's leadership, with Dunér to pay special attention to the geognostic

* As to the whole project, see: N. Dunér and A. E. Nordenskiöld, Förberedande Undersökningar rörande utförbarheten af en Gradmätning på Spetsbergen. K. Svenska Vet. Akad. Handl. Bd. vi. No. 8. In 1891 a Swedish committee was appointed to reconsider the question, and a further scheme was drawn up by Professor Rosen and published as a pamphlet in 1893. It has now been decided by the Swedish Academy of Sciences that the scheme shall be carried out, perhaps in conjunction with Russia, and expeditions to that end are to be sent to Spitsbergen in 1898 and following years.

MERIDIAN ARC

observations. The result of these efforts was the suggestion of three different meridian-arcs: (1) along the west coast from South Cape to Vogelsang Island; (2) down the middle of the island by way of Wijde Bay, Ice Fjord, Bell Sound, and Horn Sound; (3) from Ross Island (north of the Seven Islands) to the South Cape by way of the east coast, Hinloopen Strait, and North-East Land. The third of these was the line recommended. It has, however, never been run, because the sea east of Spitsbergen is seldom easily navigable and the number of fine days are few. Moreover, in order to link together the triangles set out in Wybe Jans Water with those of Hinloopen Strait, observations must be made from a high hill in the midst of Garwood Land close to the furthest point reached by us this year from Klaas Billen Bay. Professor Nordenskiöld himself informed me that the existence of a hill commanding the necessary distant views had been to him doubtful, though he believed that they had identified as one and the same the apparently highest point of a range of mountains seen from three different points near the east coast (Svanberg, the White Mountain, and Mount Lovén). That such a mountain does in fact exist (and even more than one) was discovered and proved by us this year. The surpassing eminence of Horn Sunds Tind, dominating as it does the whole southern region of Spitsbergen, visible from the west coasts of Edges Land and Barents Land, and easily recognisable when and whence soever seen, indicated its summit as the best point for observations; but the mountain was believed to be inaccessible. It was also believed that other useful mountain peaks might exist in the interior of the south part of the island between Horn Sound and Ice Fjord, by use of which as trigonometrical stations the necessity of visiting ice-blocked Wybe Jans Water might be avoided. One of the minor purposes of Herr Gustaf Nordenskiöld's expedition of 1890 was to pay attention to these matters. He accordingly landed in Horn Sound and made a rapid journey across the glaciers and mountains between that point and the so-called Recherche Bay in Bell Sound.* He concluded that Horn Sunds Tind and the mountains of similar structure north of Horn Sound were inaccessible, and therefore could not be used as trigonometrical stations. Our discovery that Horn Sunds Tind is probably visible from the Three Crowns added greatly to its importance as a possible trigonometrical station. Thus it was now become a matter of unusual interest to discover a way to its summit.

* A translation of his interesting account of this expedition is inserted as an appendix to the present volume, by kind permission of Baron Nordenskiöld.

BEGINNING OF THE CLIMB

An easy ascent up a snow incline brought us to the rocks of the little peak in which the west *arête* of Mount Hedgehog has its lower termination. They are broken rocks, lying at a steep angle. Deep, new, hard-frozen snow filled up their interstices and made the ascent very laborious, though quite easy. From the top of the little peak we looked abroad over the sea of cloud, beneath which we knew the ocean must lie, though no trace of it was visible to the remotest horizon. The surface of cloud was generally level but undulating, the crests of its motionless waves dyed pink by the midnight sun, the troughs filled with blue shadows. Straight ahead rose the steep splintered rock-ridge to the desired summit. On our right of it stretched up a broad ice-couloir, narrowing above to a snow-saddle close below the peak, and broadening below to Hedgehog Glacier, which flows almost due south to the sea, and along whose left bank lie the row of lesser peaks forming the continuation of Horn Sunds Tind. Last year Garwood led his party up this couloir, keeping close to the rocks of the *arête* by its right (north) side. There was no better way, so we went down to the col east of our little peak, and attacked the snow-slope beyond, Garwood leading now and throughout the ascent.

I was astonished, on approaching the couloir, to hear the mountain, as it were, singing over all its precipitous face. The cause of the sound was not apparent; it resembled the noise of waterfalls. The bonds of frost were, however, strong upon the mountain and must have held it for many days in a thawless grip, so that I could not believe there was any water to fall. Once in the couloir the mystery was explained. The sound arose from a cascade of fragments of ice, varying in size from a nut to a hen's egg. We soon found out their cause and whence they came. Fine snow crystals formed in upper regions of the air, so different from the large flakes of lower levels, had been flung by the gale upon the crags. Hour after hour and doubtless day after day the bombardment continued. The flying icy dust clung to the rocks, and, being constantly added to, built itself up into feathery icicles pointing towards the wind. Where there had been a constant eddy it was shown by the changed direction of the icicles. They were only an inch or two long low down, but the higher we climbed the larger we found them to be, till near the top they became splendid plumes eighteen inches long or more and of the loveliest forms, like ostrich-feathers glittering with diamond dust. It was these icicles, detached from above by the leverage of their overgrown length, and smashed into smaller fragments as they fell, that filled the air with the sibilant, rushing sound which seemed like the noise of many waters. Throughout the ascent we had to run the gauntlet of these missiles, and were often hit, and hit hard, but never so severely that it mattered. They were not big enough to knock us out of our steps, whilst, once they had taken their first bound from the rocks, they kept close to the slope, so that they seldom flew by at a level higher than our waists.

Last year Garwood had escaped this particular annoyance, but instead had found the couloir in a rotten condition with soft snow lying upon ice, so that he had to cut steps through the snow into the ice from the very start. This year, the snow being hard-frozen, step-cutting did not commence till some way further up. Garwood started with hopes that much of it might be avoided by scrambling up the rocks of the *arête*, but the ice-covering on them rendered that impracticable, or, at the least, highly dangerous. Across the foot of the couloir stretched two of the inevitable deep crevasses or *bergschrunds* which every couloir boasts. Under the conditions they were, of course, well bridged, and presented no difficulty. Bonds of frost likewise held the rocks together, so that not a stone fell across the route of our ascent. In warm weather, and especially after midday, falling stones must be very common here, nor do I see how they can be avoided, for they rake every possible line of ascent.

Once really in the couloir, step-cutting became necessary, at first mere slicing of the frozen snow, but all too soon laborious hacking into hard blue ice. We kept close to the rocks and could sometimes advance a step or two by jamming the foot into the crack between rocks and ice. Such relief was rare. I calculated that Garwood cut altogether five hundred ice-steps in the couloir. This does not include snow-steps below it or on the final ridge. Garwood made them small and far apart, whilst I enlarged them into regular shelves to last against our return. The view, when we turned round to look at it in breathing intervals, was restricted, for the walls of the couloir shut out everything except the prospect over the cloud-covered ocean, which remained from hour to hour bathed in the pink light of sunset or sunrise. The sun flung the blue shadow of our peak far out upon the cloud-floor. When we were fairly high up, the shadow of the summit became tipped with red, which, as we mounted higher, developed into a series of four concentric rainbows, apparently lying on the clouds in the remote distance and haloing the shadow of the peak. This effect, as may well be believed, was remarkable enough; but even more unusual, to my eyes, was the appearance of what I can only describe as two radiantly white roads of brightness, stretching directly away from us straight out to the horizon, one on either side of the mountain's shadow, and each making an angle of about 37°, with a line from the eye to the centre of the rainbows, or 143° round from the sun. All the rest of the cloud-floor was still mottled in blue and pink, though the pink was now growing faint, and the general tone was becoming blue-grey; the two "roads" alone were snow-white by contrast.

The higher we rose the steeper was the couloir, the harder the ice, and the greater the cold. The distance from the glacier below steadily increased; to look down upon it was like looking down a wall. The distance to the skyline above did not seem to diminish correspondingly. We came to the point where Garwood had led his companions on to the rocks last year. We, however, kept on up the ice. Then we were level with last year's highest. It had been estimated at about eighty feet below the summit, as far as the fog enabled a guess to be made; now in perfectly clear air we saw that very much more than eighty feet remained to be climbed. A strip of rocks, above on our right, descended into the couloir from the final snow *arête* at its top. We cut a long staircase diagonally across to them up a yet steeper ice-slope than any before. They proved to be nothing worse than rather steep screes encumbered with ice. We scrambled up them to the final ridge, a real knife-edge of snow of the giddiest description, for on the other side the mountain wall plunged vertically, as it seemed, 3000 feet down into the floor of cloud below. Here we entered the sunshine, and the view toward Edges Land burst upon us, but we scarcely looked at it. There was not a cloud in the sky; we should see it better from the top, and to that our attention was anxiously turned. It was still 100 feet above our heads. A thread-like snow-ridge of astonishing delicacy led steeply up to the final tooth of rock. Carefully we advanced, planting our feet on the very crest of the ridge, which had to be trodden down before it was broad enough to stand upon. Here and there overhanging cornices had to be avoided; but only care was required, there was no real difficulty. In a few minutes we touched the foot of the summit rock. It was a plumb vertical wall, perhaps fifteen feet high. I suppose we might have climbed straight up it, but an easier way was found. The rock was cloven in half from top to bottom by a crack just wide enough to squeeze through sideways if we expelled our breath and made ourselves thin. On the other side of it was a ledge giving easy access to the highest point, on which we laid our hands with a great feeling of joy. The ascent had taken five hours from the foot of the couloir.

To express the beauty of the view that now surrounded us surpasses my powers. A bare statement of its character and extent is all that I shall attempt to set down. The lowlands, bays, and wide glaciers were alike buried beneath the floor of cloud, so that much of the geographical information which else might have been obtained was withheld. Only in the south-east was there

VIEW FROM THE TOP

any sea or coast-line visible, an appearance of low-lying flat land, which may indeed have been merely a shadow upon water. The whole of Edges Land was in cloud, but Barents Land was sharp and clear, with all its peaks quite distinct and easy of identification, had one but known what to identify. Here, too, the waters of Wybe Jans Water were disclosed with the sunshine lying brightly upon them, and the long east coast of Spitsbergen leading in that direction. Everywhere else were only peaks rising like golden islands out of a silver sea. A row of such, the tops of a range of hills, ran close by us down the middle of the land towards the South Cape. In the north was a chaos of peaks, those near at hand lying in north and south rows, but the remoter ones dotted about on no discoverable plan. We identified the peaks about Bell Sound, and Mount Starashchin at the mouth of Ice Fjord, but of hills more remote we could be sure of none. So much for the distance and background of the view; its great glory, however, was in the craggy ridge of Horn Sunds Tind itself, along which we looked both to north and south. Southward it sank rapidly, but in the opposite direction it reared itself into successive jagged peaks rising out of a narrow zigzag ridge of precipitous rock. Alas! we were not on the highest point; that was now seen to be the splendid needle further north, divided from Mount Hedgehog by a deep gap, and perhaps surpassing it in height by as much as forty feet. All the rocks of this glorious ridge were covered with ice-feathers, whereon the sun shone with great brilliancy, whilst a bold shadow clothed the whole west face of the mountain. The zigzagging of the ridge brought the bright and shadowed sides into alternate prominence, and led the eye agreeably along to the sudden jut of the culminating needle. How beautifully this wonderful group of bold, snow-decked crags was enframed by the bright effulgence of the cloudy sea and its emergent islands any one can imagine better than I can say. The effect on the spectator was heightened by the sense of standing high and alone, for, save along the knife-edged ridge, the mountain fell from our feet with such utter abruptness as to seem everywhere vertical, so that we had the sensation of looking from a balloon rather than of standing upon the solid earth.

We now observed that a very fine range of peaks, striking inland northward from the west side of Horn Sound's north bay, is the orographical continuation of Horn Sunds Tind, the sound itself having been cut right through this ridge. No visitor to Horn Sound can fail to notice the remarkable end peak of this ridge, which rises from the sea, a rock-blade of the narrowest description, one side very steep, the other plumb-vertical. Numberless birds nest in the lower part of its cliffs, inaccessible alike to men and foxes.

Tearing ourselves away from the summit and its entrancing view, when at last we were almost frozen stiff, we retreated a few yards down the east face into a little hollow, sheltered from the wind and open to the tepid sun. There a frugal luncheon was eaten and pipes duly smoked, and there we left our cards in a crack, for there were no loose stones out of the snow wherewith to build a cairn, nor, if there had been any, was there room enough on the summit for a cairn to stand. In such raw atmosphere, however, motion is needful for enjoyment, so that neither of us was unwilling to commence the descent. Garwood's notion of traversing the whole length of Mount Hedgehog's summit-ridge to its north end and descending by another west *arête* from that point was silently abandoned. With the mountain in good condition it might be accomplished and enjoyed, but the iced rocks made the attempt not worth consideration. By the way that we came up by the same must we return.

Trotting down the *arête* to the top of the ice-covered screes was easy enough, but from that point the greatest care was required. Both of us afterwards confessed that we looked forward with trepidation to the descent of these screes, for they were very steep, very loose, and slippery with powdered uncompacting ice. Descents, however, are generally worse in prospect than in actuality, and this was no exception. We hardly realised where the bad place was till it had been passed; but at the foot of the rocks there lurked a quite unforeseen perplexity. Our beautiful ice-staircase had so completely disappeared that for some time we could not discover its position. The steep snow-covered ice-slope was absolutely smooth. No visible inequality broke the evenness of its white surface. With some difficulty I found our old footsteps on the rocks. Standing in them and leaning downward, whilst Garwood held the rope, I probed in all directions for the topmost ice-step. It seemed as though an entirely new staircase would have to be cut. But at last luck revealed the missing hole, which, like all the rest below, was filled up and smoothed over by snow-dust and ice-fragments that had fallen into it. I cleared it out and began the descent. The next step was similarly masked and had to be sought and cleared, though, of course, its position was more easily found. The steps, having been cut as far apart as we could stride, were difficult to reach down to, nor did we venture to tread down a pace till the exact position of the foothold had been discovered. Sometimes new steps had to be cut because the old ones were beyond reach of the axe. It was interesting work which prevented the return from being monotonous, but rendered progress rather slow. When the *bergschrund* was approached difficulties were at an end. We looked back and found the summit again enveloped in cloud, whilst the sea-fog below was steadily rising. Before we had quitted the rocks of the peaklet at the foot of the ridge we were well into the dense mist, where, in a few yards, we promptly lost our way and had to appeal to the compass for direction. Garwood's cairn was reached a few minutes later, and our remaining provisions were consumed under its shelter. The descent to camp was without incident. Tired and hungry, we reached it after an absence of fourteen hours, and were delighted to find that the violence of the waves had abated.

It may be of interest to Alpine climbers to compare this ascent with that of some known peak in the Alps. The height of the mountain from the foot of the glacier is about 4500 feet. From the *bergschrund* at the foot of the couloir to the top is about 3000 feet. The ascent, therefore, from the point where the climb commences is somewhat longer than, and happens to be very similar in character to, the corresponding part of the ascent of the Aiguille Verte* in the Mont Blanc range, made by way of the south-east couloir. Horn Sunds Tind, indeed, may be compared in other respects with the Verte group. Mount Hedgehog represents the Verte itself, the west *arête* corresponds to the Moine ridge, whilst the highest northern needle resembles the Dru, both

* The summit of the Aiguille Verte is 3700 feet above the Jardin.

in position and in form. Some day, no doubt, it will be climbed, though I scarcely think Garwood and I shall return to climb it. Horn Sound appears to be a bad weather region, and we have had enough of its inhospitable shores.

About 7.30 P.M., after a good sleep, we awoke to find the most glorious drama of colour playing for us upon the sound. Already, through ten hours of every night, when thin clouds covered the sky, marvellous long-drawn-out sunset effects brooded over the southern extremity of Spitsbergen. Day by day they were creeping further north, heralds of the long winter night. What we saw that evening was no ordinary sunset of the temperate regions merely extended in duration, but such a sombre splendour as might fitly usher in the fiery consummation of the world. The hidden sun, level with a low, thin roof of cloud, shone both upon its upper and lower surfaces, painting the under-side a ruddy brown. Peculiar and unexpected reflections made lights in strange places. The mountains were dark chocolate or rich purple in colour. Lighter chocolate were the glaciers. The fjord was dark-green, shot with pink reflections from above. Away beyond the sea was a belt of clear sky beneath the cloud-roof. Overhead, pink clouds, rent and twisted by some high gale, writhed in an island of blue in the upper regions of the air. New snow whitened the lower hill-slopes.

CAMP MOVED

Chilly blasts came and passed, telling of the winter that was at hand.

Late in the evening we breakfasted and packed up camp. Soon after midnight the boat was easily launched in the calm bay. It was our intention to row to the far side of the head of the sound, where there were rocks that Garwood thought might prove worth examination. No sooner, however, was the point of Goose Bay rounded than a strong wind from the north-east met us, against which we could not make headway. Close at hand was a little cove, well protected by rocks, and there we were compelled to land, just forty-eight hours before the steamer was to call and fetch us away.

The doings of these two days are not worth record. They were a time of low clouds and frequent heavy rains. No exploration could be done, because nothing could be seen. We made useless expeditions to Kittiwake Glacier; we scrambled among the Stonehenge Rocks, and otherwise killed time. Thick clouds and the dipping sun made the nights so dark that candles had to be burnt in the tent during several hours. The sea became quite calm; birds seemed to increase in numbers upon the water, as though they were gathering in Horn Sound for their southern flight, just as the whaling fleet in old days used to gather either here or in Bell Sound.

Early on the morning of the 21st, Nielsen called us with news that the *Lofoten* was in sight. To pack our baggage and launch the boat was the work of a few minutes. We rowed out to the steamer, which took us and our goods on board and promptly headed away for the open sea and the south. As Horn Sound was quitted, the weather temporarily improved. For a moment the clouds broke or lifted, and showed us, for the first time, all the height and width of Horn Sunds Tind—a sight to us most interesting, but not specially impressive in the dull illumination that prevailed. We passed the South Cape at sunset and enjoyed one memorable last look along the west coast, whose peaks and promontories were visible as far away as the Dead Man at the mouth of Ice Fjord. The northern horizon behind them was striped with ruddy and golden radiance. The under side of the everlasting cloud-roof was strangely illuminated with delicate pink light, reflected up to it from the white surface of the interior of Spitsbergen, upon which the low sun contrived to cast its rays just below the northern edge of the cloud-cap—an effect I have never before observed. I have several times seen the underside of Spitsbergen's cloud-roof shining pink, and always supposed that it reflected direct sunshine; but probably in such cases a preliminary upward reflection of the light from a snowfield may be assumed.

Our voyage was delightfully calm. We saw many whales and hundreds of seals in schools, especially near Bear Island, north-west of whose south point we cast anchor for a few hours in the afternoon of the 22nd. The top of Mount Misery was buried in a soft grey cloud, but the splendid cliffs below were close at hand, with pillared rocks jutting out of the sea at their feet. A heavy swell broke upon the barren island, casting towers of spray aloft. Off shore blew a stiff local breeze that made landing a wet and laborious process, for it was only just possible to row against it. Every one who landed returned to the ship drenched to the skin.

A few miles away from Bear Island the wind dropped and the sea was calm. From hour to hour the temperature rose, so that those of us who had spent any length of time in Spitsbergen felt that we were coming into luxurious and almost tropical latitudes. About sixty miles north of the North Cape two ships under full sail came in sight far away over the calm sea. They were bound from Arkangel, laden with timber for English ports. When they had been left behind, the hills of Norway appeared along the southern horizon. Their low line gradually rose from the bosom of the waters as we approached. The sun foundered into the sea about nine o'clock, just when our ship passed under the North Cape's beetling cliff and rounded into the sheltered eastern bay, where is a little landing-stage at the foot of a zigzag path leading up a gully to the plateau above. Bay and gully were shrouded in the gloom of evening, but the air was warm and rich with the smell of the land. We rowed ashore, a motley international company. Something like a race was started for the summit of the Cape, which is about 1000 feet above sea-level and a long distance from the landing-place. I see that Bädeker gives seventy minutes for a rational ascent; we most irrationally did it in twenty-eight. It was a merry party that gathered on the top—Belgians, Poles, Hungarians, Swedes, English, Norwegians, men of science, seamen, travellers. Nansen's *Fram* crew were represented by three of its members, including the laughter-loving giant, Peter Hendriksen, every one's butt and playfellow. Bottles were uncorked, and their contents shared round. Rocks were prized down the cliffs. It was a gay hour. Though heated by the uphill race, we could sit without chill on the exposed promontory; for the air to us was full of southern warmth, and felt like the air of hot Italian valleys to a man descending into them from the Alps.

The party soon dispersed, and I found a secluded corner, under the very point, with the northern ocean below. "In such moments Solitude is invaluable; for who would speak, or be looked on, when behind him lies all Europe and

Africa, fast asleep, except the watchmen; and before him the silent Immensity, and Palace of the Eternal "—thus thought Teufelsdrökh, as he stood on this particular spot one June midnight, clothed in his "light-blue Spanish cloak" and looking "like a little blue Belfry." "Silent Immensity and Palace of the Eternal!"—the words are not too strong for the wonder of that view. There was no midnight sun to look upon; a spot of brightness in the midst of the orange and crimson north showed where, far beneath the horizon, it was looking abroad over the cloud-covered arctic world. The delicate crescent of the new moon beamed not far away, with a single planet near it. Straight from my feet plunged the splendid cliff to the measureless stretch of the Arctic Sea. In the east, air, ocean, and clouds merged together in a harmony of tender violet, so soft, so rare of tint, that the eye, once turned thither, was loath to wander again. A faint low promontory of land, dividing sky from sea, lured the fancy onward to the regions of romance—Novaja-Zemlja, the Kara Sea, and the way of the North-East Passage. Not thitherward was our way, but home. By noon we were again in Hammerfest.

CHAPTER XI

ON THE USE OF SKI

SINCE Nansen published his book, "The First Crossing of Greenland," the English public has known of *ski* and their use. Ski (pronounced *shee*) are Norwegian snowshoes, now admitted to be the best form of snowshoe in the world. They are long, narrow planks for fastening one under each foot, so as to distribute over an area of soft snow, many times larger than the area of the foot, the weight of a man walking. They not only prevent him from sinking into the snow, but, if it is in suitable condition, they enable him to slide along on its surface. The common idea in England is that the art of using ski is very difficult of acquisition. This, as I shall show, is a mistake. No doubt the almost miraculous expertness attained by the best Norwegian and Swedish skisters (to coin a needed word) is beyond reach of ordinary Englishmen, who take to the sport when they are full grown and have rare opportunities for practising it. But for purposes of mere travel far less skill is required.

In fact, it is with skiing as it is with skating.

SKI FOR EXPLORERS

Any person, with normal habits of exercise and control over his limbs, can learn to skate in a few days well enough to go straight ahead over good ice at a tolerable pace. Within a fortnight of his putting on skates for the first time, he might go a-touring along frozen Dutch canals without being much, if anything, of a hindrance to a companion, the most expert of figure-skaters. To pass the St. Moritz test as a figure-skater takes months or even years of practice, but that is to learn the art, not the mere craft of skating. So it is with skiing. The artist skister can race down steep slopes at an appalling velocity, leaping drops or crefts of almost incredible dimensions. A traveller who needs ski for the purpose of exploring the great snowy areas of the world has no occasion to acquire skill of that pre-eminent character. He is not called upon to advance faster than a sledge can be dragged by men or dogs, as the case may be, and that he can learn to accomplish in a very short time. Sliding downhill is a little more difficult; but any climber, who can make standing glissades with facility, soon learns to glissade on ski down any ordinary slope of snow.

When Garwood and I landed in Norway last year, we had never seen a pair of ski, and did not know where to buy or how to choose them. During the summer we travelled over 150 miles on ski, dragging our sledges behind us. Later on we went to Stockholm and saw all manner of ski in the Exhibition there, and availed ourselves of every opportunity that came in our way to obtain information about ski and everything connected with them. We soon learnt that there are ski of all sorts and kinds. They differ in the material of which they are made, and they differ in form. I am told that ash is the best material to make them of. The points to be seen to are the straightness of the grain and the absence of knots. Lightness is less important for a traveller than strength.

The questions of form and size are determined by the purpose for which the ski are to be used. Speaking generally, narrow ski are faster than broad of the same area. In soft snow, however, the advantage vanishes, for narrow ski sink in more deeply than broad; indeed, for very soft snow, ski require to be both broad and long. The edges and the hinder ends may be either rounded or cut off square. For hill climbing it is certain that the squarer the angle of section of edges and hinder ends the better, seeing they take a better hold of the snow, and prevent sliding sideways or backwards; sharp edges also make steering easier on hard snow. Relatively short, broad ski, are best for hill climbing, and, in general, for the work of a traveller. They are easier to advance on, easier to steer, and easier to turn round with. Their length may be anything from two to one and a half metres, two metres for choice; they should measure eight centimetres at the narrowest

TELEMARK SKI

part under the foot, increasing forward to from nine to ten centimetres at the broadest part, just where the toe of the ski begins to turn up. The front ends should be well turned up, the points being raised from twelve to fifteen centimetres above the level of a horizontal plane on which the ski stand. Such ski are of the Telemark type, and can be bought under the name "Telemark ski," from the Scandinavian manufacturers. A good pair, made of selected ash, costs about fifteen shillings.

The most important matter for a novice is to learn how best to attach his ski to his feet. There are various ways in which this can be done. In all alike the attachment is such that the foot can be freely bent and the heel raised, while the fore part of the foot is kept firmly in contact with the ski. The roughest attachment is a mere loop or strap of leather, fastened to the two sides of the ski, and gripping the front part of the foot. This, however, permits the foot to wobble, a most disagreeable condition for a beginner. Such fastenings were all that Nielsen and Svensen used, and they seemed quite comfortable with them. The common binding, and the best for a traveller, is more complicated. The broad strap, going over the fore part of the foot, is divided longitudinally on each side about the level of the sole. Through the two loops thus formed there passes a stout piece of cane covered with leather, the middle of which goes round the back of the foot near the heel, whilst the two ends are brought forward and drawn together in front of the toe, where they are fastened down firmly to the wood of the ski. This fastening has to be adjustable, so that the cane loop may be drawn close against the heel. There are several sorts of adjustment; one is shown in the illustration. Another, per-

haps better, is a kind of vice that opens and shuts by a screw; it grips the two ends well and enables either of them to be pushed forward ahead of the other. A small strap, sewn on to the back of the boot, low down, holds the cane in place. The same result may be less well attained by using an additional strap that passes both under and above the instep, and is sewn on both sides to the leather covering of the cane. This form of attachment is usually employed by winter skisters in the Alps. For advancing over level ground, all the fastenings may be loose; but for hill climbing they need to be tight, so that the feet are firmly attached to the ski and can direct them with certainty. Beginners will certainly find tightly-attached ski much easier than loose to walk or glissade on.

The next question is that of footgear. For moderate cold, such as you meet with in summer in the arctic regions, ordinary climbing boots do well enough ; but leather Lapp shoes are better. These seem to be known by different names. I

find them called "pjäxa-schuhe" in a Swedish-German catalogue, which mentions two qualities, Norrbotten (price 8s. 6d.), and Norwegian (price 14s. 6d.). A particular kind of band is made, called a pjäxband, a kind of putti, for winding round the top of the boot to keep out snow.

Within these leather boots thick goathair stockings should be worn. So far as I know, they can only be purchased in Norway and Sweden, the price varying according to the length. For very great cold, such as that of arctic winter, shoes of reindeer fur, stuffed out with hay, are required. The adjustment of ski to these is a less simple matter, for if the hay is badly packed the cane is likely to rub against the heel and produce a painful raw.

One more part of the equipment for skiing has yet to be mentioned. It is the staff. Racing skisters use two sticks, one in each hand, but for glissading the two have to be held together like a single staff. To facilitate this, there are specially constructed staves made to fit together. The ordinary ski-staff is provided with a kind of plate near the spike, to prevent the point penetrating too far into soft snow, and to give resistance for a push off. Travellers using ski in mountain regions will probably find it best to carry an ordinary ice-axe and make shift with it. An axe is far less convenient than a longer bamboo staff, for mere purposes of skiing, but its other uses, when ski are laid aside on steepening slopes where real climbing is required, overbalance its obvious defects. It would be easy to devise some form of small, circular plate to slip over the point of the axe a little way up the stick, and wedge there, quickly removable when the axe is required for step-cutting.

The skister's equipment is really simple enough, but its various parts are not easily purchasable in England. The following manufacturers of ski showed exhibits at the Stockholm Exhibition of 1897 : Helmer Langborg, 6 Birger-Jarlsgatan. Stockholm (who also sells the various

SKI MANUFACTURERS

kinds of boots, goathair stockings, gloves, pjäxbands, &c.); L. H. Hagen & Co., of Christiania; L. Torgensen & Co., of Christiania (who also make arctic sledges); Langesund Skifabrik, Langesund, Norway (a very good exhibit); Fritz Huitfeldt, of Christiania (gold medal at the principal Norwegian show for ski). I give this list of names quite ignorantly, just as I copied them down. I have no knowledge about the estimation in which they are held, their relative expensiveness, or anything else concerning them. One or two of these firms issue priced catalogues, which, I suppose, may be obtained on application. Ski are also made and sold in Austria; they will be found advertised in the publications of the German and Austrian Alpine Club. Ski of this make are sold in winter at the chief Alpine centres, but they are very inferior to ski of Scandinavian manufacture.

Little need be said about how to learn the use of ski, but one or two hints, even from so poor a performer as the present writer, may be suggestive to an absolute novice. The first desideratum is to fasten the ski properly to the feet, so that the boards run truly with the feet, not with an independent motion of their own. The trouble at first is to keep the two ski constantly parallel with one another, and in the direct line of advance. People whose habit is to turn out their toes in walking, however slightly, will find themselves constantly impeded by that trick. To keep the ski parallel, the feet must be parallel. The motion is not one of walking but of shuffling. The ski are not raised from the ground, but merely pushed forward, the knees being kept bent, and the action resembling a sort of easy run. If the snow is in good condition, the ski will slide forward a little at the end of each step. The use of a staff or a pair of staves is to prolong the distance of this sliding. If a staff is used it is grasped in both hands and thrust into the snow on one side every time the foot on that side is advanced. If two staves are used, one in each hand, each is thrust back (like a walking-stick) against the snow, turn about, the left when the left foot is advanced, and *vice versâ*. Another way is to take three quick steps and to thrust with both staves at the moment of the fourth step. Yet another trick is to thrust with both staves at every third step; this changes the foot each time, but is more difficult. About four miles an hour is an average kind of pace on the flat with fairly good snow. Fifty kilometres in 4h. 20m. 17.5sec. was, I believe, the record for flat racing two or three years ago.

The ascent of hills on ski involves new problems. If the snow be soft enough for the ski to sink into it about half-an-inch, and if the slope be gentle, there is no difficulty in walking straight up. If the slope gradually and steadily steepens, there will come a point at which the ski no longer hold, but slide backward when the weight of the body is thrown upon them. The beginner must then zigzag, pressing the edge of the ski into the slope but, otherwise advancing as on the flat. This is easy enough; the trouble comes at the angles of turning, where his legs are almost sure to slide asunder, or he will tread with one ski on the other. In turning round, even on the flat, it is at first no easy matter to avoid fastening one ski down by treading on it with the other. You should begin turning by moving the foot which is on the side towards which you are going to turn; keep the legs well apart and make the rear ends of the ski the approximate centre of rotation. In turning round on a hillside it is easier to turn with the face, rather than the back, towards the hill. Another way of walking uphill in suitably soft snow is to turn the toes well out and lift each ski over the other; this is more difficult than zigzagging. In very steep places neither method can be applied; you have to advance sideways with the ski kept horizontal, an easy but slow method of progression.

Downhill the real fun begins, and the difficulty of maintaining the balance becomes serious. The weight must be thrown forward, the knees kept bent, and the staff, or pair of staves held as one, used as in glissading. The ski must be kept strictly parallel and close together, with one foot a little in advance of the other. The problem is to adjust the balance to every varying degree of slope and alteration in the slipperiness of the snow. Such alterations have to be foreseen and prepared for. The beginner must expect to fall often on hands and knees and to sit down with undesirable frequency when he leasts expects. He will find it much easier to fall than to rise again. He should practice glissading on a gentle slope, then on a steeper. Slopes that he finds too steep for direct descent can be negotiated by zigzags, but much time will be lost at the turns.

Whether ski could be advantageously used in summer in the Alps is doubtful. The ascent, still more the descent, of Mont Blanc between the Grands Mulets and the Vallot Hut would certainly be facilitated by them, but they are unsuited even for a broad snow-*arête*. Agreeable, however, as ski would be on any snowfield, and valuable as a protection against concealed crevasses, they are far too heavy to be carried by a mountaineering party for incidental use. Still they might be employed with advantage in certain places. For example, if a party of climbers were to make the Concordia Hut the centre for a week's climbing, they could not do better than provide themselves with ski. Thus equipped, all the surrounding mountains, anywhere between the Lötschenlücke and the Oberaarjoch, would be brought within their easy reach. The new Monte Rosa Hut would likewise be an excellent ski centre, and so would the Becher Hut by the Übelthal Glacier in the Stubai Mountains of Tirol. For winter climbing in the Alps ski have already established their utility. I understand that several of the easy Oberland passes, such as the Strahleck, have been crossed on them, whilst at lower levels their value is even more obvious. Whether ski-running will ever attain in western and central Europe the rank as a sport which it holds in Norway and Sweden is a question that only the future can decide.

CHAPTER XII

GEOGRAPHICAL RESULTS

BEFORE taking leave of the reader it seems advisable to indicate briefly the general geographical results of our two seasons of exploration in the interior of Spitsbergen, and to state what is now known about the structure of the surface of one of the most interesting areas of arctic land. On Nordenskiöld's chart, the best map of Spitsbergen existing at the time when we began our labours, both Garwood Land and King James Land are described as covered with "inland ice." Now, if the phrase "inland ice" merely means glaciers, so that it may be correctly applied to the glaciers of any district of snow-mountains, such as the Alps or Caucasus, it is a useless phrase, and ought to be abolished. Most persons of whom I have inquired receive from it a different impression, and judge it to be descriptive of a complete and continuous icy mantle enveloping a whole country, as Greenland, for instance, is enveloped. In fact, Nansen, in his book on Greenland, always uses the term "inland

NEW FRIESLAND FROM HINLOOPEN STRAIT.

INLAND-ICE 207

ice" to describe the great interior ice-covering. "Ice-sheet" is apparently a better descriptive term for such a mantle, and I shall accordingly so employ it. The term "inland-ice," being essentially vague, should, I think, be erased from geographical literature, or only used as an indefinite term for the land-ice of an unexplored region, the exact nature of which is unknown. As long as a flowing body of land-ice is contained within definite watersheds and mountain ranges, it is a glacier and not an ice-sheet. The juxtaposition of no matter how many glaciers does not form an ice-sheet, but merely a glacial area. It is necessary to be thus particular in definition because, as has been stated above, neither Garwood Land nor King James Land, nor any large part of Spitsbergen, except New Friesland and North-East Land, is covered by an ice-sheet. They are all merely glacial and mountain areas. The discovery of this fact is the principal geographical result of our second expedition. That it is a not unimportant result I now proceed to demonstrate.

The old theory that glaciers not only polish but systematically excavate their beds is practically abandoned. Its supporters naturally considered that the larger the mass of ice the more vigorous would be its excavating action. A great arctic ice-sheet was regarded as an extraordinarily powerful excavator. We now know that moving land-ice does not so operate upon its bed, but, beyond polishing the surface of the rock it covers, has mainly a conservative effect upon it. In the case of a country like the interior of Greenland, wholly buried under ice, the buried land-surface undergoes modelling to a very slight degree, except round the coast. On the other hand, in the case of a glacial region, where mountains rise above the mean level, and where rock-faces are exposed to the rapid denudation that takes place at all snowy elevations, great developments of surface-formation are going forward. In the case of an ice-sheet, the forces acting on the land-surface are conservative; in the case of a glacial region, the acting forces are formative. Hence the immense importance of clearly distinguishing between these two types of ice-bearing country.

Without pausing to describe the particular places or views in Spitsbergen that suggested particular conclusions to my mind, let me rather, for briefness, indicate how it seems to me that one or two well-known mountain groups in Europe have been acted on by glaciers—for instance the Mont Blanc and Bernese Oberland ranges. Both, in their present developed condition, have been carved out of more solid masses which may be described as originally wrinkled plateaus, the original wrinkles having been approximately parallel to their length. Of course the denuding forces, whatever they were, operated simultaneously with the elevating forces; but the two may be considered separately for convenience' sake, and we may speak of the plateau as first elevated and afterwards denuded. It must, however, be understood that during the earlier stages of the elevating process, water, not snow and frost, was the denuding agent. The culminating point of each plateau was approximately in the position of the highest point of the present ranges. The original main drainage must have run along the lines of the wrinkles; now, in both cases, it runs at right angles to that direction.

In order to indicate my meaning, it is not necessary to reconstruct entirely the original form of the plateau and its lines of drainage; one or two instances will suffice. In the case of the Mont Blanc range,* I suggest that originally there was a glacier with its head near the present summit of Mont Blanc, having for its left bank a ridge (or plateau-edge), now represented by the Aiguille du Midi and other *aiguilles*, the Aiguille Verte, the Aiguille du Chardonnet, and the Aiguilles Dorées; whilst its right bank was approximately coincident with the modern watershed as far as Mont Dolent, except between Mont Blanc de Courmayeur and the Tour Ronde, where it has been denuded away. This ancient drainage

* Herr Imfeld's new map is the best on which to examine this theory.

system has been broken down, and now the snows of the upper reservoirs are all discharged by such glaciers as the Mer de Glace or the Glacier d'Argentière, which cut across one or other of these old containing ridges or plateau-edges. Similarly with the Bernese Oberland, I suggest that the original crinkled plateau was drained along depressions approximately parallel to its length, whereof one was a high glacier basin with its head near the top of the present Finsteraarhorn and flowing W.S.W. over the Grünhornlücke and the Lötschenlücke and down the Lötschenthal. The old watersheds to right and left of this glacier have been driven back by the general disintegration of the plateau-edge, and broken utterly down in various places, so that its snows are now drained away at right angles to its direction by the Great Aletsch and Walliser Viescher glaciers.

In fact, in these cases it is with the glacial drainage as in the Himalayas it is with the rivers. When the great Asiatic plateau was elevated, whereof Tibet alone retains anything approximating to the original surface condition of the whole, the drainage ran off along the hollows in the line of the crinkling of the surface coinciding with the strike of the strata. Now, however, by the operation of rivers eating their way back into the plateau at right angles to the strike of the strata, all the great rivers flow at right angles to their original direction. The Indus was originally a stream no bigger than the Swat River, flowing down the edge of the elevated region. It ate its way through the Nanga Parbat range into the depression which goes on to Gilgit, and thus it stole all the waters of the upper Indus of to-day, which in the remote past, I believe, discharged themselves (over a high region since excavated into mountain ranges) into the Kunar River, and before that into the Oxus. Similarly the Gilgit River has eaten back through the Rakipushi range and stolen the waters of the Hispar-Hunza valley; and the Hunza stream has eaten back through the Boiohaghurdoanas range, and so reached the Kilik Pass. It is noticeable that, in each case, the river has broken its way through a range in the immediate proximity of its highest peak, that is to say, just where the fall and gathering of snow has been greatest and the denudation most energetic.

In the case of rivers the eating back process is well recognised and understood. It is not really the work of the river, but it is accomplished by the various forces of atmospheric denudation, by frost and thaw, by avalanches and so forth, all taking place about the head-waters of the stream. I suggest that, under the action of similar forces, glaciers likewise creep back, and that the modelling of snow-mountains out of high plateaus is largely due to this process. According to this theory, though glaciers do not excavate their beds to any great extent, they widen them by carrying away the results of atmospheric and other denudation, and similarly they eat back at their heads. The most striking examples of this process I have seen are in Garwood Land. There, far in the interior, are a series of cliffs, several hundred feet in height. What the origin of these cliffs may have been is immaterial to the question under consideration. They form the front of the remains of the old plateau, which is being and has been eaten away. At the foot of the cliffs are the snowfields of the great glaciers which flow thence in a south-east direction to the head of Wybe Jans Water. By the melting of the snows above the cliffs and on their ledges, and by the action of frost and thaw, the rocks are rapidly broken up. The *débris* fall upon the glaciers below, and are carried away. If there were no glaciers in this position, the *débris* would pile up, a slope would be formed, and would presently reach up to the top of the cliff, and protect it from further denudation. The presence of the glaciers below prevents the *débris* from collecting. The cliff thus continues its existence, and merely moves backward by a steady progress, just as the cliff retreats over which Niagara falls. Where weaker rocks are encountered, or denudation is locally more energetic, the cliff eats backward more rapidly. An embayment is formed, which tends both to widen and to creep backwards, be-

BLUFFS OF THE SASSENDAL.

coming in time a tributary valley. Of such valley heads which have crept back into the plateau we saw several examples; one in particular I remember in the midst of King James Land, which had annihilated a portion of a mountain range dividing two great glaciers, and had thereby caused what had originally been the chief *névé* basin of one of these glaciers to drain into the other instead of down its own tongue. When two neighbouring embayments, reaching back from the lower level into a plateau, send arms to join one another, or meet obliquely, a nunatak is formed. The nunatak near our farthest point in Garwood Land was produced in this manner.

Keenly possessed by the memory of these phenomena, I went recently to Grindelwald, and was immediately struck by the resemblance in character between the great bluffs of the Bernese Oberland—the Eiger, Mettenberg, and Wetterhorn—and the bluffs of Spitsbergen's Sassendal. The latter, as we know, were formed, and are still in process of development, by means of the torrents draining the snowfields above, which eat away the plateau and cut back into it, thus carving out a row of flat-topped steep-fronted hills that jut forward into the ever-widening main valley. It seemed evident that the ancient Oberland plateau had been similarly cut down, the excavation not having been accomplished by the grinding action of glaciers pushing forward and filing down their beds, but by the action, first, of torrents, before the plateau was elevated above the snowline, afterwards of glaciers; both torrents and glaciers creeping backwards at their heads, where faces of rock are exposed to rapid atmospheric denudation, and the *débris* that fall are transported to low levels by the movement of the flowing ice.

It was thus, I suggest, that the Upper and Lower Grindelwald glaciers and the Rosenlaui Glacier invaded the plateau and crept back into the heart of the mountain mass, isolating as high individual peaks the Wetterhorn and Schreckhorn. Originally they were "corrie glaciers," plastered on to the north face of the plateau—just such glaciers, in fact, as is the Guggi Glacier, which lies in the hollow between the Jungfrau and the Mönch. They have crept farther back than it, because they had the better start, but the Guggi Glacier now emulates their former vigorous initiative. The cliffs at its head are being continually broken and worn away by the action of frost. The rocks that fall from them either tumble on to the *névé* and are carried down or roll into the *bergschrund*, and so get under the ice, where no doubt they are ground to dust, and may do some excavating in the process. That, however, can only be in the upper regions; lower down, the waters below the glacier are the excavating agent, rather than the glacier itself, except, perhaps, at the edge of some subglacial cliff beneath an icefall. In this way the

THE GREAT ALETSCH GLACIER 215

rocks of the north face of the ridge between the Jungfrau and Mönch are being eaten away, and the ridge itself is not merely being lowered, but its crest is being pushed backward towards the south. Every yard of its movement is made at the expense of the Jungfrau Glacier. Let the process go forward for a sufficiently long time, and the area now occupied by the upper basin of the Jungfrau Glacier will be occupied by a snow-basin lying at a lower level, and draining northward down the Guggi Glacier.

Similar, I suggest, was the development of what is now the Great Aletsch Glacier. Originally, according to this theory, the Lötschen Glacier stretched back to the Finsteraarhorn, and had for its left bank a ridge parallel to, but south of, the range of which the Aletschhorn is now the culminating point. The Aletsch Glacier's original head was on the south face of this range, but the glacier ate its way backwards, its head advanced to the north, finally broke its way right through the range and drew off a portion of the ice of the Lötschen Glacier.* The snout of the Lötschen Glacier was thus disconnected from its former *névé*, and a pass (the Lötschenlücke) was formed between them. The *névé*, at what is now called the Place de la Concorde, flowed as a great icefall over the remnant of the old left bank of the original glacier. It no doubt deepened and widened

* The Walliser Viescher Glacier was similarly employed.

the breach, and, as it did so, lowered the level of the snow in the upper reservoir, whose various branches were thus likewise enabled, each in its place, to creep backwards at the expense of the plateau. In this manner were formed the Ewig Schnee Feld, the Jungfrau Firn, and the other *névé* tributaries of the present great glacier. The great icefall gradually diminished in turbulence as the cliff beneath it was broken and rounded away, till now it is merely represented by the crevassed area just below the Concordia Hut.

If there is any truth in the theory thus briefly propounded, in a form which must be considered altogether incomplete and preliminary, it follows that the distinction I have endeavoured to make between an icesheet and a congeries of glaciers is a distinction of the first importance; for under an icesheet none of the processes are going forward which are vigorously proceeding in a glacial region. The old idea of Spitsbergen was that its interior consisted of a great icesheet, fringed at the edge by a number of boggy valleys and green hillsides. Our explorations have shown the utter falsity of this conception. Let me now briefly indicate the outlines of the true geography of the main island.

Whether at one time the whole island was enveloped in an icesheet which was gradually withdrawn from the west towards the east, or whether the west part of the island has merely

SPITSBERGEN GEOGRAPHY 217

been longer raised above the sea than the east part, I do not attempt to determine. At any rate, it seems to be a fact that the forces of denudation have been longer at work, or, at least, more vigorously at work, all down the west part of the island, and that the resulting mountain formation is most developed in the west, and becomes continually less developed as you proceed toward the east. All down the western region you find highly specialised mountain-forms —peaks and ranges of considerable abruptness and marked individuality. As you advance eastward the mountains become generally more rounded, till the original plateau-form, and even parts of the undenuded plateau itself, are encountered.

Bearing in mind this general structure of the land-surface, it will now be easy to describe the character of different parts of the main island. The whole of the north coast, as might be expected, bears evidence of a more rigorous climate than districts further south. This was speciallly noticed by us when proceeding down Wijde Bay, at whose mouth the snow lay down to sea-level in the month of August, whilst, twenty miles in, the snowline was almost 1000 feet above sea-level. The northern rim, therefore, may be regarded as a separate geographical division. At the north-west angle of the island is a region of very bold mountains and large glaciers. It is well represented by the beautiful and often described Magdalena Bay. Nothing is known about the interior south-east of it, but some old Dutch charts mark a valley leading from the extremity of Mauritius or Dutch Bay up to a sequestered lake in the hills. Whether the draughtsman intended his winding valley and river to represent a glacier and the lake a snow-field, or whether a true lake and river existed here in the eighteenth century, can only be settled by some one going to look.

Passing southward down the west coast, we come to the seven parallel glaciers ending in the sea, known to the whalers as the Seven Icebergs. These all appear to flow down from a high common snowfield which stretches east toward Wood Bay and south almost to the head of Cross Bay. South-eastward this high plateau is broken by a series of *névé*-valleys, the chief of which discharge themselves towards Ekman and Dickson bays. Their general direction is south-south-east. South of this plateau region comes the mountainous area of King James Land, whose character has been described in this volume. The main watershed runs north and south. A series of parallel glaciers drain south-south-east from it to Ice Fjord. The valley system on the west is less regular, but the glaciers are equally numerous and fine.

The deep north-and-south depression filled by

SPITSBERGEN GEOGRAPHY 219

Wijde Bay and Dickson Bay is bordered on the west by a range of mountains, a group of which intrude between and divide the bays. Some of these are of striking form, but no one has ever been amongst them or accurately determined their position. East of the two bays comes the plateau region. Its edge is cut up by a few deep valleys, down which the icesheet of New Friesland sends glacial tongues to Wijde Bay, but east of Dickson Bay the marginal valleys are longer, and no glaciers come out of their mouths. The portion of the plateau between Dickson and Klaas Billen bays is a good deal cut up by deep valleys, such as the Rendal, the Skans valley, and the Mimesdal (all well known to geologists), but there are no large glaciers found upon it. Further east comes a great glaciated area approximating to an ice-sheet in appearance, but with many exposed faces and peaks of rock. From it several large glaciers flow into the sea, namely, the glacier that ends in the head of East Fjord of Wijde Bay, the glacier that fills a wide valley debouching into Hinloopen Strait opposite the South Waiigat Islands, some more glaciers that empty into Bismarck Strait and that neighbourhood, the series of great glaciers at the head of Wybe Jans Water, and the Nordenskiöld Glacier (specially explored by us) near the head of Klaas Billen Bay. All these glaciers are divided from one another by more or less well-marked watersheds.

The neck of Spitsbergen, which may be defined as bounded on the north by a line from the mouth of Nordenskiöld Glacier to Wiche Bay, and on the south by the Sassendal and the depression across to Agardh Bay, is a district that would well repay exploration, and is easily accessible from the Post Glacier at the head of Temple Bay. Nowhere are better illustrated than here the phenomena of mountain formation by plateau degradation under the action of rivers and glaciers. In the east are the remains of an ice-sheet; in the west are deep and wide glacier and river valleys. Between the two are many mountain ranges, and some peaks of considerable height and abruptness.

A line drawn from the head of Van Keulen Bay to Whales Bay forms the southern limit of the next region to the south—the region that I call Adventure Land, using the old name which in the case of Advent Bay has been clipped of its last syllable in the present century. It is a country of boggy valleys, rounded hills, and relatively small glaciers. Originally it was one large plateau formed of soft, almost horizontally bedded rock, except along its west margin. It has therefore been penetrated by wide valleys radiating in all directions and cut down almost to sea-level. A range of rather fine peaks lies along the west coast; behind them are some large glaciers descending north into Green Harbour and south to the mouth

SPITSBERGEN GEOGRAPHY

of Low Sound. Then the undulating country begins. Several valleys lead inland from Coles Bay, whilst from Advent Bay starts the Advent Vale with its many branches. From Low Sound a series of boggy valleys strike in to north and south. At the north angle of its head opens the deep valley of the Shallow River (after the Sassendal the largest valley in Spitsbergen), whose upper part has never been explored. The eastward prolongation of Low Sound, which was known to the Dutch as Michiel Rinders Bay is very poorly charted, but we know that at its north angle there is a secluded inner harbour, with a big ramifying valley leading back from it, while at its extreme east corner three large glaciers debouch together. One of these probably connects by a high snowfield with the head of Strong Glacier descending to Whales Bay.

Last comes the south division of the island, over which we had a panoramic view in 1897 from the summit of Mount Hedgehog. Unfortunately a roof of cloud covered the glaciers, and we could only see tops of mountains rising clear above it. The north-west angle of this region was explored in 1897 by Mr. Victor Gatty,* who found it to consist of a ring of snowy mountains surrounding the *névé* of the Fox Glacier, which discharges into the so-called Recherche Bay. A gap or col, south-east of Dunder Bay, separates

* *Alpine Journal*, vol. xviii., p. 501.

this group from a range of hills running for some distance south along the coast, and called Roebuck Land. The extremity of these hills abuts against the right foot of Torell Glacier, one upper bay of which rests against the hills immediately south of Recherche Bay, whilst another stretches inland to the east as far as the main watershed of the island. There are one or two other approximately north and south ranges of hills lying west of this watershed. East of it the plateau-character resumes its predominance. The southernmost part of the island, south of Horn Sound, is dignified by the boldest mountain range in the country, that of the Hornsunds Tinder, which lie west of the watershed, and run almost due north and south. East of them are at least two lower parallel ranges, beyond which the ice-covered country seems to dip to the sea.

Of the other islands in the Spitsbergen group, North-East Land is the largest. It is known, from Baron Nordenskiöld's exploration, to be covered with a true icesheet, the edge of which descends to the sea all along the south-east coast. The north coast and the small islands off it altogether resemble the northern belt of the west island. The west belt is a low undulating region, from which the icesheet has retreated in relatively recent times.

In the sea east of Spitsbergen are two islands whose existence has long been known. They were named Wiche Land, after an old navigator. Walrus hunters have landed on them, but they were first really explored in 1897 by Mr. Arnold Pike.* The west island, now called Swedish Foreland, has a high flat-topped backbone. The east island, King Karl's Land, consists of two hills, about 1,000 feet high, united by a low flat isthmus. There is no ice-sheet on either island and only small unimportant glaciers.

I have never landed on Barents or Edge Islands, though I have seen them from east and from west. Neither possesses an icesheet. Both are practically devoid of glaciers down their west coast, and have large glaciers in the east. The whole of the south-east of Edge Island is occupied by a great glacier ending in the sea. Barents Land has several sharply pointed peaks, but the Edge Island hills are mainly flat-topped, like those along the east coast of the main island.

Prince Charles Foreland now alone remains to be considered. It is very badly represented on the existing chart. At its southern extremity is an isolated hill. Then comes a very flat plain of about fifty square miles, raised but a few feet above sea-level. North of it is a mountain range consisting of fine, sharp snow-peaks. It is cut off on the north by a deep depression, running in a south-west direction from Peter Winter's Bay, which, though marked south of St. John's Bay on

* Vide *Geographical Journal*, 1898.

the chart, lies some miles north of it. North of Peter Winter's Bay and Valley the mountain range is continued; but the peaks, though fine in form, are not so high as those of the south group, but they send down eastward an almost uninterrupted series of glaciers into Foreland Sound. Further north are yet lower snowy hills, which end in the bold headland called Bird's Cape or Fair Foreland.

FAREWELL.

APPENDIX

Account of Herr G. Nordenskiöld's Traverse over the Glaciers from Horn Sound to Bell Sound in 1890.*

June 15th, 1890.—At six o'clock in the evening we landed by boat at the foot of Rotges Mount at a spot where a small valley gave access to the mountain above. We imagined that on the other side of this mountain we should meet with the smooth inland ice and that it would extend all the way along to Bell Sound. After taking a hurried farewell of our comrades, we buckled on our ski, put our knapsacks on our backs, and commenced our course up the little valley. When we reached its highest point, however, we found that it was connected with another valley which led down to Horn Sound. We were therefore obliged to climb the face of the mountain on the north side of the valley, which was extremely laborious, because the snow was frozen so hard that we could not use our ski on the steep slope. One

---

* Translated by the Rev. E. Shepherd from Herr G. Nordenskiöld's paper, *Redogörelse för den Svenska Expeditionen till Spetsbergen 1890*, published in *Bihang till K. Svenska Vet. Akad. Handl.* Bd. 17, Afd. 2, No. 3, pp 10–17.

of us went in front and stamped holes for the feet in the hard crust—tough work in which we constantly relieved each other. The rest followed in his steps. At midnight we had mounted a ridge, uniting two summits, and here we rested for an hour. The temperature of the air was 28° Fahrenheit and the altitude 994 feet above sea-level.

We continued on the 16th in a northerly direction, but were obliged to stop again after a few hundred steps, because a thick mist shrouded the whole landscape. When, after a little while, this cleared off, we hurried up and descended the other side of the ridge towards a huge glacier. Down this we made good speed and in a short time were close to the smooth snow-slopes. The mountains in this district are built up of the so-called Hekla-Hook strata—hard slates, quartz, and dolomite. The mountains which belong to this system always possess much more precipitous and wilder outlines than those which are built up of the softer rocks belonging to newer formations. Many of the former are probably extremely hard or perhaps impossible to climb; for example, Hornsunds Tind. This is probably the case with many of the steep-pointed peaks around the wide expanse of snow over which we travelled. They gave the landscape a wild and desolate beauty.

In the north, on the other side of the glacier, lay another mountain range with several lofty summits. In the west a heavy bank of fog obscured the view the whole time. Probably the sea would be visible in this direction in fine weather. Sometimes the fog-bank was driven up the glacier by the wind, and enwrapped us so completely that we were obliged to retreat for a time. In the east numerous summits were visible, and the glaciers in this direction did not appear to be connected with the inland ice. The snow-mantle which covered the glacier-ice was perfectly smooth; there was not even a spot to break the dazzling whiteness, not the smallest unevenness on which the eye could find a resting-place. This accounted for one under-rating the distances in this district more than usual, as happened to us in the case of the mountain on the southern (? northern) side, because we thought we only had before us a snow-covered sloping valley, not worth thinking about, which from its depth could not possibly take more than half an hour to traverse. In reality it was only after several hours' walking that we gained the summit of the opposite ridge.

It was long after midday on the 16th when we reached that summit. The height above the sea at the spot where we crossed was only 2215 feet, but on the east and west were several considerable heights. We attempted to scale one of these which lay nearest to us on the east, so as to obtain an uninterrupted view over the country; but, after we had with great difficulty dug a few hundred steps in the hard surface and crept up so far, it was found impossible to go any farther. We were then 2457 feet above sea level and could easily recognise again from this point the highest point of Hornsunds Tind. The mountains to the west of us seemed to be of considerable height and also easy to ascend. In the north the snow-covered ridge on which we were fell almost precipitously down to a considerable glacier. We were therefore obliged to make a little to the west before we could begin our descent.

Even here the slope was steep and covered with a

crust, hard and shining like ice, so that our advance became pretty dangerous to our necks, and ended in our losing our balance and rolling down the slope at top speed without being able to stop. After we had happily reached level ground, collected ourselves, and gathered together our widely scattered baggage, we set forward over the glacier. It sloped gently downwards and promised a connection with the wide field of inland ice in the north-west. A little further down the glacier the outlook became more extended. We had now only a few kilometres left to the inland ice proper,* which spread out before us like a level white sheet bounded in the distance by blue peaks. Late in the evening we put up the tent and rested a few hours at the edge of the glacier. After a long search we were lucky enough to discover water on a slope. It was the first water we had seen since leaving the coast. As it was so early in the year we found neither pools nor runlets on the surface of the glacier. Our supply of spirits was rather scanty and only sufficed for warming up our food, not for melting the snow; hence, while travelling over glaciers and the inland ice we suffered much from thirst, and were often compelled to eat snow, which is said to lower the strength considerably.

On *June 16th* we rose at 11 P.M., and began our journey over the inland ice proper. The temperature of the air was 31° F. The weather was lovely, not a cloud was visible in the sky, and the atmosphere was wonderfully clear. We first passed a number of mighty moraines, which were heaped up where the smaller glacier joined the inland ice. At the very brink of the latter

* The *névé* of Torell Glacier.

flowed a small brook. The surface of the inland ice itself was perfectly even, covered with fairly hard frozen old snow. No crevasses could be distinguished along the whole of our route, and only in a few places did slight hollows betray the existence of such.

We first went toward some high mountains which rose out of the ice some kilometres distant. They formed the spurs of a range of mountains, running north and south, which continued up to the end of the mountains at Cape Ahlstrand, east of Recherche Bay. In the west, along a width of more than ten kilometres, the inland ice opened into the sea (it bears the name of Torell Glacier). In the east the horizon was bounded by the inland ice. To the north-west it extended, shut in between two mountain chains, unbroken to Recherche Bay, to whose large glacier it joins on. That was the way we took.

After some hours' journey, in the early morning of the 17th we reached the foot of the mountain mentioned above, which forms the southern point of the eastern range of mountains. At the foot of the mountain we found several small watercourses, and therefore chose this place for a halt. A large number of fallen blocks at the mountain's foot afforded a strange sight. The part of the inland ice from the east here joined that from the north. A bank of gravel, which stretched like a black streak towards the west, probably formed the middle of the moraine. The height above the sea at this point was 358 feet.*

After some hours' rest we continued north-west over

---

* 109 metres. From the context it seems certain that this should be 309 metres, = 1014 feet.

the inland ice, which was smooth in all directions and free from crevasses. We had already been a long time out on the endless white plain when, at nine o'clock in the morning, we pitched the tent to get a little sleep. The height of our resting-place above the sea was 1011 feet. We had walked by night because, notwithstanding that the temperature does not rise above 39° F. in the shade, the heat when the sun was high was quite unbearable. After midday signs of a change of weather appeared, and heavy clouds began to rise behind the mountain summits. We hastily got up again, but after a few hours' walking we were enveloped in a dense mist. We continued, however, for some hours, steering our course by a pocket compass which we had brought with us. On the night of the 18th we stopped because we feared to make our way among the northern coast mountains, which could not be very far distant from us now. All the spirits were finished, and our store of provisions was by no means abundant.

Next day (19th) we tried to advance toward the coast in spite of the fog, which had lifted at intervals and given place to a heavy snowstorm, a terrible hindrance to our progress. The snow was very wet and fastened in large lumps on Björling's ski, which were not covered with sealskin. Our ski, too, which had been stripped of part of their skin-covering by the hard snow-crust, slid very heavily. Björling preferred to go on foot and carry his ski on his back, but he found this pretty hard work. We soon noticed that we were already quite amongst the mountains and, after searching about for a long time in the fog for a way forward, we finally came to a halt, recognising the necessity of waiting until it lifted somewhat.

We set up our tent near a steep snow-slope, evidently leading down into a broad valley. As it drew on towards evening the fog lifted a little. Right down in front of us spread a broad valley, apparently the continuation of a bay. In the south-south-west there appeared to be sea, and in the north we thought we could also see the water. I thought that the bay in the north-west was Dunder Bay, and that we must have strayed somewhat too far to the west. Our provisions were scarce; there would only be sufficient to last the four of us one day; it was therefore necessary to find the ship without delay. Björling, partly on account of the unfitness of his ski, was thoroughly exhausted and was unable to travel any farther. I therefore determined to leave him in the tent with the sleeping-bags and the remaining stores, and with Erikson and Joakim, unencumbered by impedimenta, to endeavour to reach the ship and thence send to rescue Björling. The way to the ship however was longer than we supposed, for the *Lofoten* did not lie in the harbour in the inner part of Recherche Bay as I had expected. The bay being ice-packed, the ship lay off Cape Lyell, a circumstance which added a good ten kilometres to our distance.

It was only after nine hours' unbroken march, tired and hungry indeed, that we reached the *Lofoten*, and our way would certainly have been longer still had we not, after walking a few hours almost due east, thought we could see water on the horizon, and so were induced to take a more northerly course. After we had followed this direction for a time, Erikson declared he could see a ship in the distance. Our joy was great when I ascertained with the field glass that three masts were visible a long way off to the north. The ice over which we had passed was continuously smooth. Only the last few kilometres nearest the sea were very full of crevasses, generally covered by snow-bridges, which we could cross on our ski without difficulty. Luckily for us the ice on the inner harbour of Recherche Bay was strong enough to bear, so we avoided a long detour.

We continued on the other side of the bay to Cape Lyell over a large glacier, terminated in the north by a precipitous ice-wall, below which begins a wide expanse filled up with moraines and cut up by numerous crevasses. We did not see this precipice at first from above, and were nearly falling over it on our ski, but just managed to pull up at the last moment. After following the edge of the glacier for a good distance to the west, we at last succeeded in finding a place where a snowdrift had built a bridge upon which we could get down. At last we stood on the beach, and only a couple of gunshots off lay the *Lofoten*. Firing our revolvers and shouting loudly, we aroused the captain's attention and were soon safe on board. It was six o'clock in the morning of the 19th.

My first care was to send some men back to rescue Björling. Unfortunately it was several hours before any one could start. Klinckowström had gone away in one of the boats with part of the crew to the east side of Recherche Bay, hoping to meet us there. A message was sent off to him immediately, and his boat's crew were soon on board. Klinckowström offered to go himself with two men to rescue Björling. The three skisters were soon ready for their journey. As they

APPENDIX

rowed in a light boat to the bottom end of Recherche Bay they shortened the way considerably. Following the west side of the bottom of the glacier between the mountain and the ice, they found ski tracks which they endeavoured to follow right up to the tent. After an absence of about six hours they returned. They had been able to follow the tracks for about a couple of hours or so, but the snow, which had fallen heavily high up among the mountains, had stopped them completely. Under such circumstances nothing remained for them but to turn back with their errand unaccomplished. There was however no very great reason for anxiety, for the sleeping-bags and provisions enough for one man for several days had been left in the tent.

It cleared up again a little on the 20th, so I sent off Joakim, who had been my companion and consequently knew the position of the tent; two men accompanied him. On the morning of the 21st one of them came back with the news that they had certainly found the tent but that Björling had left it. They had found a card with this communication—that "after waiting in vain for one and a half days he had started with all possible speed to the west beach of Recherche Bay." He had however clearly mistaken Dunder Bay for this, and started in quite the wrong direction, as his tracks plainly showed. Joakim followed up this track while the other two returned on board. I now sent a boat round Cape Lyell to Dunder Bay to meet Björling there. Joakim, after following his track for a distance, had overtaken Björling who was on his way south; he came back then with the boat, and on the afternoon of the 21st we were all together on board again.

APPENDIX

The ski expedition thus described shows that the inland ice of West Spitsbergen differs considerably from that of North-East Land as well as of Greenland. It consists in this (at least at the time of year when we undertook our expedition), namely, a perfectly level tract covered with snow without any of the crevasses and mounds which generally make expeditions over glaciers and inland ice so dangerous and difficult. Glacier-rivers, fountains, and glacier-lakes, which are so often met with in Greenland, are here altogether absent. Similar formations are also wanting in North-East Land's inland ice, but its surface is more uneven; crevasses and channels are very common. This circumstance—viz., the fact that the inland ice of West Spitsbergen seems to be very much easier to traverse than glacier ice in general—gives a certain importance to the plan of measuring an arc of meridian in this district, a proposal which has been suggested several times. A number of triangulation points ought to be established on the mountains, which are surrounded on all sides by the inland ice. This might have been thought to be very difficult, but, far from proving an obstacle, the inland ice forms a capital medium for connecting the points of triangulation. To convey instruments and equipment on proper sledges for some tens of kilometres over this smooth surface would surely be no very severe task.

A few remarks are called for by this pleasant account of a very interesting little expedition. The inland-ice referred to was not any part of an ice-sheet and in no wise resembled the ice-sheets of Greenland and North-East Land. It was merely the snowfield of Torell Glacier, which consists of two great arms, one coming from the north and reaching to the watershed behind Recherche Bay, the other from the east, where it is limited by the main mountain-backbone of the island, the orographical continuation of the Hornsunds Tinder. The time of the expedition being the month of June, the glaciers and snowfields were still deeply covered with winter snow, which buried the crevasses out of sight. Later on, no doubt, there would be no difference in character between Torell Glacier and the Nordenskiöld and other glaciers explored by us. The same waterlogged snow, the same large lakes, the same deep and broad torrents, must be formed in all the glacial regions of Spitsbergen. Hence it follows that the month of June is specially favourable for expeditions over glaciers in this part of the world, for then the chief impediments to progress have not been formed, the weather is likely to be fair and the surface of the snow to be hard and smooth. Unfortunately it is not till the end of June that, under present steamship arrangements, the island is cheaply accessible. An exploring party desiring to land upon Spitsbergen at the end of May could only do so by coming up in a vessel specially hired to bring them.

INDEX

Advent Bay, 1, 67, 90, 121, 126, 154, 221
Adventure Land, 36, 121, 220
Agardh Bay, 220
Ahlstrand, Cape, 229
Andrée and his balloon, 155
Atmospherical phenomenon, curious, 180

Baldwin, Mr., 67
Bar, The, 70
Barents Land, 28, 46, 47, 183, 223
Barrel-vaults of ice, 51
Bear Island, landing on, 191
Bernese Oberland, glacier action in the, 210, 213
Birds Cape, 224
    Nesting-places of, 3, 50, 65, 79, 98, 108, 133, 143, 165, 184
Blomstrand Harbour, 71, 145
    Mound, 71, 145
Boat, troubles with our, 167
Bornemisza, Baron, 154, 155

Calving of a glacier, 13, 74, 77, 140, 141
Chydenius, Mount, 28, 43
Clouds, low-lying, 63, 104, 113, 131, 138, 140
Coal Bay, *vide* Coles Bay Haven, 71, 147
Coles Bay, 68, 221

Cookeries, whaling, 151, 160, 162
Crevassed glacier, 16, 77, 110, 133
Crevasses, Depth of, 143
    Difficulties with sledges amongst, 16, 132, 133
Cross Bay, 10, 71, 151, 218
    Mountains, 104, 122, 131
Crowns, The Three, 72, 85, 109, 116, 119, 120
    Ascent of one of, 119
    Glacier, 72, 105, 114, 122

De Geer Peak, 21, 22, 23, 48, 50
    Ascent of, 27
Deceptive appearances on snowfields, 24
Deer Bay, 71
Diadem Peak, Ascent of, 124
Dickson Bay, 33, 39, 218, 219
Dubbin, Norwegian and other, 49
Dunder Bay, 221, 231, 233
Dutch Bay, 218

Eating-back rivers and glaciers, 210, *et seq.*
Ebeltoft's Haven, 151
Edge Land, 223
Edlund, Mount, 28, 41
    Ascent of, 42
Eiderdown, 65

INDEX

Ekman Bay, 73, 92, 116, 121, 218
Ekstam, Herr, 1, 67
Elevation of the land, 59
English Bay, 69, 70, 85
Equipment, 18
Exile Peak, 124
Expres, The, 2, 154

FAIR Foreland, 224
Falling ice, 177
Fleur-de-Lys Point, 5
Fog on snowfield, Puzzling effect of, 31
    Travelling through, 21, 31, 32, 33, 34
Foreland, Prince Charles', 68, 122, 223
    Sound, 68, 122, 224
Fox Glacier, 221
Foxes, 88
Fram, Crew of the, 2, 192

GARWOOD, E. J., 1, and *passim*
    Land, Description of, 56, 57, 58, 212, 219
    Land, Wide view over interior of, 38, 46
Gatty, Ascent by Mr. Victor, 221
Glacier, Ice-tunnel in a, 137
    Phenomena, notable, 51, 111, 128
    Torrents, 79, 83, 103, 106, 111
    Cliffs, 9, 77, 141
Glaciers, Action of on their beds, 207
    Advance of, 138
    Calving, 13, 74, 77, 140, 141
    Ending in deep water, 10
    Ending in shallow water must advance, 11
    That eat back at their heads, 60

Goose Glacier, 159, 168, 170, *et sqq.*
Haven (Horn Sound), 157, *et sqq.*
Islands (Ice Fjord), 64
Green Harbour, 220
Greenland and Spitsbergen, Contrast between, 36, 61

HEAT on the snowfields, 87, 100, 108, 130
Hedgehog, Ascent of Mount, 170
Heley Sound, 44
Highway Dome, 91
    Pass, 90
Himalayas, How rivers have " eaten back " in the, 210
Hofer Point, 158
Horn Glacier, 166
    Sound, Visit to, 157, *et sqq.* 225
    To Bell Sound over Torell Glacier, 225, *et sqq.*
Hornsunds Tinder, 121, 165, 170, *et sqq.* 222, 226, 227
Hyperite Hat, 67

ICEBERGS, 141, 142, 145, 147
Ice-encrusted rocks, 178
    Flat below a glacier's foot, 160
    Honeycomb, 19, 55, 81
    Sheets, 36, 37, 206, 207, 216
Inland ice, 206, 234

KING James Land, 89, 96, 218
King Karl Island, 223
Kings Bay, 70, 138, *et sqq.*
    Landing in, 74
King's Highway, 72, 76, *et sqq.*, 115
    Expedition up, 76, *et sqq.*
Kittiwake Glacier, 165
Klaas Billen Bay, 5 *et sqq.*, 48, 55, 62, *et sqq.*, 219

INDEX

LAKES, Burst Glacier, 53, 100, 137
Lerner, Dr., 3
Lovén Islands, 72, 141, 143
    Mount, 45
Low Sound, 221
Lyell Cape, 231
Lyktan, 33

MAGDALENA Bay, 218
Mauritius Bay, 218
Meridian arc in Spitsbergen, Proposal for measurement of a, 173, 234
Michel Rinders Bay, 221
Mimesdal, 7, 17, 219
Mitra Hook, 71, 152
Moraines, Struggle with sledges up and over, 15, 80, 134
Mount Blanc Range, Previous form of, 209
Mountain exploration, Difficulties of, 95
Mountains, Scale of, 91, 118

NEW Friesland, 207, 219
Nielsen, Edward, 22, 32, 84, 125, 127, 131, 141, 170
    Mount, 76, 78
Nordenskiöld, Baron, A. E., 41, 156, 174, 222
    Herr Gustaf, 176, 225
    Glacier, 6, 8, *et sqq.*
Nordenskiöld Gl., Expedition up, 15, *et sqq.*
North Cape of Norway, 191
North-East Land, 207, 222, 234
Nunataks, 38, 84

OSBORNE Glacier, 98, *et sqq.*

PALÆOLITHIC climbing, 163
Peter Winter's Bay, 69, 223
Pike, Mr. Arnold, 158, 223
Plateaus carved into mountain ranges by rivers and glaciers, 57, 208
Post Glacier, 220

Pretender Pass, 104
    Peak, 73, 85, 105, 107, *et sqq.*
    Scramble on, 113
Prince Charles Foreland, 68, 122, 223
Prismatic Ice, 102
Pyramid, The, 7

QUADE Hook, 70
Queens, The, 73, 85, 101, 104, 105

RECHERCHE Bay, *vide* Schoonhoven
Reindeer, Destruction of, 9, 144
Roebuck Land, 222
Rotges Mount, 225
Russian trappers, 69, 151, 159

SABINE, Sir Edward, 173
St. John's Bay, 68, 99, 223
Sassendal, 213, 220, 221
Schoonhoven (Recherche Bay) 221, 222, 229, 231
Scoresby, Dr., 71
Scoresby's Grotto, 145
Screes, 114, 119
Seven Icebergs, The, 218
    Islands, 154
Shallow River Valley, 221
Shoes, Lapp, 49
Silence of the snowfields, 89, 123
Skans Bay, 3, 219
Ski, 24, 30, 34, 37, 55, 93, 100, 106, 123, 125, 127, 129, 194, *et sqq.*, 230
    Fastenings of, 197
    First attempts on, 25, 201
    Footgear for, 199
    Glissading with, 203
    In the Alps, 204
    Kinds of, 196
    Makers of, 200
    Records with, 202
    Staff for, 200

Sledges, Misfortunes with, 55, 79, 80, 103, 132, 139
Snow blown by a gale, 35
Snowfield, Different aspects of surface of, 94, 98
  Travelling over, 21–50
  Waterlogged, 82, 102, 124
Snowshoes, Canadian, 26, 30, 32, 49
  Norwegian, *vide* Ski
Spitsbergen, Geography of, 217
Stonehenge Rocks, 164
Stones, Falling, 110
Storm on a snowfield, 34, 35
Strong Glacier, 221
Svanberg, Mount, 43
Svensen's troubles, 23, 32, 34, 35, 36, 40, 48, 50, 66, 84, 101, 119, 129, 149, 153, 156

TEMPLE Bay, 220
  Mount, 66
Terrier Peak, 18, 30, 47, 50, 52
Teufelsdrökh on North Cape, 193
Thordsen Plateau, 3, 28, 93, 219

Tibet, Partially undenuded plateau of, 210
Torell Glacier, 222, 228, *et sqq.*, 235
Tourists in Spitsbergen, 1, 67, 155
Trevor-Battye, Mr. A., 157

VIEWS, Notable, 6, 17, 19, 23, 28, 33, 38, 46, 48, 71, 87, 92, 105, 112, 114, 120, 126, 136, 140, 144, 177, 180, 182, 192

WEATHER, Bad, 22, 34
Whales Bay, 221
White Mountain, 41
  Ascent of, 45
Wiche Bay, 220
  Land, 45, 158, 223
Wijde Bay, 29, 39, 122, 217, 219
Winter, Approach of, 136, 166, 171, 180, 188, 189, 190
Wood Bay, 218
Wybe Jans Water, 28, 39, 41, 43, 46, 47, 183

ZEEHONDE Bay, 69

www.ingramcontent.com/pod-product-compliance
Lightning Source LLC
Chambersburg PA
CBHW032006230426
43672CB00010B/2263